ROCK PLANTS FOR
SMALL GARDENS

Tiny plants have a fascination all their own, but all too often, although they are at home in the rock garden proper, it is difficult there to appreciate their full beauty without an unconscionable amount of stooping. It should be remembered that they can, for instance, be swamped by their larger neighbours, and hardy though they are, they do sometimes require a little extra attention to give of their best.

Accordingly they are often grown in sinks either of natural or artificial stone, in troughs or in pans, in scree beds and frames, peat beds, the raised beds known as 'billiard tables', and in rock pots. It is with these forms of cultivation that Royton E. Heath deals.

Although he lists and describes over 1,000 suitable plants, his book is no mere catalogue of names, for every aspect of culture from the construction and planting of the various receptacles to the propagation of plants is dealt with in detail.

Mr Heath, a connoisseur of this type of plant and its cultivation, has aimed at satisfying the needs both of the novice and of the more advanced gardener and to this end he describes not only the more usual plants but also the rarer ones which, though perhaps difficult to track down, are obtainable in this country.

ROCK PLANTS
FOR
SMALL GARDENS

ROYTON E. HEATH
F.L.S., F.R.I.H. (N.Z.)

COLLINGRIDGE BOOKS

Published by Collingridge Books,
and distributed for them by
The Hamlyn Publishing Group Limited
London · New York · Sydney · Toronto
Astronaut House, Feltham, Middlesex, England.

First published in 1957 under the title
"Miniature Rock Gardening"
by W.H. and L. Collingridge Limited.
Second edition, under present title, 1969
Third edition, 1982

ISBN 0 600 36811 4

Printed in Great Britain by Hazell, Watson and Viney Limited,
Aylesbury.

Dedicated to my friends of the
Alpine Garden Society
Multum in Parvo

ACKNOWLEDGMENTS

I would like to acknowledge the kind assistance of many people. Space only allows me to mention a few, but to my many friends of the Alpine Garden Society who have given me facilities to take notes and photographs of their plants and troughs, my thanks are due. Individually, Miss Jean Turner for photographs of troughs and sinks, the late Mr F. V. W. Sedgley for the outstanding line-drawings, and lastly my wife for her infinite patience in cleaning up faded specimens and notes.

CONTENTS

ILLUSTRATIONS

Line-drawings

Colour Photographs

Black and White Photographs

9

INTRODUCTION

In writing this introduction, I am very conscious of the public interest in this subject. During recent years in no other sphere of gardening has so much progress been made as in that of the cultivation of rock and alpine plants. The Royal Horticultural Society's flower shows, the leading county shows and even the local horticultural societies invariably include classes for rock plants in their schedules, while the two international societies, the Alpine Garden Society and the Scottish Rock Garden Club, are showing yearly increases in their membership. Chelsea Flower Show, always the pointer of gardening fashions and trends, draws huge crowds of professionals and amateurs alike, all seeking the new and also the old choice flowering plants.

But why is it that the focal points, for many gardeners, seem to be the stands devoted to the showing of alpine plants? Is it because the dainty, delicate, bewitching charm of these wildlings, mostly unspoilt by man's handiwork, creates a reaction in the beholder, who is for ever asking this question of the nurseryman, 'Will it grow in my garden?' Of all the questions most widely asked I think that this stands high, but the answer is not so easy for unless conditions of soil, aspect and position are known no straightforward answer can be given, yet there *is* an answer, and this is trough and miniature gardening. Here conditions can be artificially produced to suit the catholic tastes of these delightful miniatures, at the same time providing a new means of gardening even to town dwellers whose sole gardening area consists of a few yards of paving or concrete slabs. This does not mean that the more fortunate cannot indulge, for these troughs and miniature gardens look delightful flanking a lawn or arranged on a terrace adjacent to the house; what is more beautiful than an old country cottage of local stone which has a collection of these miniature gardens constructed of the same material, filled with choice flowering rock plants all blending into one harmonious picture?

Unfortunately, some alpines are not easy to grow in the rock garden owing to our ever-changing climate, but in troughs where conditions are more under the control of the cultivator, the majority can be grown successfully over a number of years. The specialist can arrange his plants in botanical order if he is so minded, using separate troughs for different genera; for example, a collection of Kabschia saxifrages in one, silver saxifrages in another and sempervivums (houseleeks) in yet another. This method of cultivation not only provides a beautiful effect of the different species and varieties within the genus, but allows the specialist to satisfy his ego by growing a collection of plants all of one family together.

Unless used with the greatest care the dwarf and slow growing conifers are not easy to place in the rock garden, often giving it an unnatural look, but in troughs they add that touch of character which is so necessary and desirable in this type of gardening, and the slight root restriction in the trough helps them to retain their dwarf stature. Although this will be dealt with more fully in the chapter devoted to these dwarfs I should like to emphasize here that all these dwarf trees must be on their own roots or gardeners will find to their cost that in a year or so the tree will have taken complete possession of the trough to the detriment of the other occupants. This will necessitate replanting the whole of the trough, possibly with fatal consequences to its occupants if they are intolerant of root disturbance.

Another aspect of this method of gardening is that each miniature trough or sink is in itself an artistic creation but, unlike a painting, it is a living thing and provides within its framework a series of delightful pictures ever changing with the passing of the seasons.

Lastly, there is a more practical side. Gardening has among its devotees a large number, dare we say a majority, of elderly people to whom stooping is a wearying and tedious business, yet who still desire to tend their plants, and what is more simple than a series of troughs arranged on slabs of stone to suit their height without the necessity of bending. Also, how much easier it is to keep off that arch-enemy of all rock plants, the voracious slug, which will completely spoil many a choice plant on the open rock garden, when use is made of troughs, scree beds and frames, peat beds and rock pots.

R.E.H.

PART ONE

CULTIVATION

CHAPTER ONE

TYPES OF TROUGH AND THEIR CONSTRUCTION

Natural Stone Troughs, Construction of Troughs from different types of Natural Stone, Construction of Cement Troughs, Small Portable Troughs, Weathering of Troughs, Scree Beds, Scree Frames, 'Billiard Tables', Peat Beds, Tufa, Hypertufa, Rock Pots

NATURAL STONE TROUGHS

IN the early days of the hobby of planting troughs and sinks it was an easy matter to obtain the real thing, especially in the districts where there were lime and sandstone quarries, for all the adjacent farms and smallholdings abounded with these troughs, many lying disused and admirably weathered in odd corners. These would be in all sizes ranging from ordinary kitchen sinks through pump troughs, horse and pig troughs to the old troughs into which the blacksmith used to plunge his horseshoes after fashioning them to size. For a few shillings and often for nothing the farmer was only too pleased to get rid of them—they were there for the taking, generally only needing two pairs of strong hands to get them into a car or van for removal to the garden. Unfortunately the demand exceeded the supply as time went by. The farmers, not as simple as they are often made out to be, found here an ever willing public eager to pay good money for this, in their minds, rubbish, so that today not only is the real thing scarce but often the price asked is prohibitive.

If it is possible, and the price is within the bounds of your purse, by all means use the real thing for there is nothing superior to it, but the substitutes with which I shall deal more fully are to my mind not only just as acceptable but have the added advantage of being tailor-made to suit the situations in which they are to be used.

Drainage. In all troughs a drainage hole is essential and this should be at the lowest end of the trough; in most cases it is already there, as in kitchen sinks, and in such cases, when setting up the trough, small wedges of flat stone must be placed under the trough till there is a slight cant in the direction of the drainage hole. Another method if the cant necessary to ensure perfect drainage will result in the trough appearing unbalanced, is to lay a coat of equal parts of sand and cement—well mixed and moistened with water until it is workable—with a trowel over the whole of the base so that the drainage hole is at the lowest point. This is a very important point for unless this is done it will result in water stagnating at the bottom of the trough and will mean the difference between success or failure.

If, as is often the case with old water troughs, there is no drainage hole, it will be necessary to make one with a hammer and hard chisel. Should it not be possible to do this yourself a local stone mason will oblige quite cheaply. Always chip towards the centre of the trough for any weakness is invariably found towards the sides. Should any cracks appear while carrying this out they are best filled with equal parts of sand and cement moistened and well worked in, after roughing up the cracks with a chisel so that the cement mixture keeps in well.

Rendering. Some of the old troughs, especially those constructed out of sandstone (limestone is a much harder material), are soft or may have worn thin in places with many years of usage. These should be given a thin coating roughly $\frac{1}{4}$ inch thick of equal parts of sand and cement mixed with water and applied with a trowel over the whole inside, thus forming a complete inner shell. Where cement is used it is always best to soak the troughs for at least 24 hours by stopping up the drainage hole and filling with water to which has been added enough permanganate of potash crystals to colour the water a deep purple. This will neutralize any harmful chemicals and acid present in the cement.

Should the real thing not be procurable for reasons of price or scarcity there are two alternatives. First, many nurserymen and gardening sundriesmen stock a large number of ready-made troughs in all sizes and shapes and at prices according to the materials used in their construction. They will gladly quote prices and sizes upon application.

HOME-MADE TROUGHS

The second alternative is to make your own troughs by one of three methods. One gets a certain satisfaction from being able to say 'I

This is an artificial trough made from Hypertufa. At the back is *Primula marginata*, *Lewisia howellii* and *Edraianthus pumilio*, and, in front, *Armeria caespitosa*, *Phlox douglasii* and *Salix × boydii*.

A natural stone trough with *Chamaecyparis obtusa nana*, on the left *Potentilla verna nana* and on the right *Campanula pilosa*.

ABOVE LEFT: A natural stone trough with, at the back, a saxifrage, *Chamaecyparis obtusa caespitosa*, *Leontopodium alpinum*, *Primula marginata* and *Gypsophila aretioides*. Towards the front are *Aquilegia glandulosa*, *Oxalis enneaphylla minuta* and *Saxifraga lilacina* and *S. baldensis*.

ABOVE RIGHT: A trough of natural stone with *Chamaecyparis obtusa nana*, *Gentiana verna* and *Salix retusa*.

BELOW: Troughs, both natural and artificial, and a low scree bed containing many dwarf flowering plants and both dwarf conifers and shrubs in a paved area.

made that myself', and in these days of high labour charges there is a considerable saving of cost besides the added advantage of making troughs to suit one's own requirements and surroundings. In this connexion, if the troughs are to be placed on a terrace constructed of the natural paving stone they should be made of this material if possible and the finished articles will blend naturally with the surroundings.

Using Walling Stone. In two of the methods of construction natural stone is used, cemented to form a whole. For the first it will be necessary to go to your local builder's yard or depot where walling and paving stone is sold and ask for anything from a few pounds to a hundredweight or so of the small pieces of either walling or paving stone which invariably collect and cannot be sold for making walls or paths. You will find that the builder will dump any amount in your

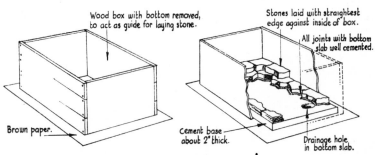

FIG. I. *Building a trough with walling or paving stone*

garden for a very small payment. I obtained over three hundredweight in this way and it formed the basis of a mixed sempervivum garden.

A wooden box without base is next constructed to the size and depth required for the finished trough, see Fig. 1. This can be made from any old material provided it is well seasoned for unless this type of wood is used distortion may occur; this applies to all wood used in the construction of troughs described in this chapter. The best method of joining the wood is to use screws, so that when dismantling after use no strain which can cause a fracture in the finished trough is put upon the work by trying to lever out nails. Another point is that the framework can be used repeatedly by rescrewing the pieces together whereas if nails are used the framework will soon be weakened. On a level piece of path or ground a sheet of brown paper large enough to protrude over the edges of the box is laid down, and the box placed on it. Next a mixture of 2 parts of sand to 1 of cement, moistened with just enough water to bind the mixture together, is laid to a depth of 2 to 3 inches—the depth will depend on the size of the trough—on the brown paper inside the box and firmed. As a rough estimate all troughs up to 18 inches in length should be 3 inches in depth. A small cork or piece of broom shank should be inserted in the corner where the drainage hole is required, and pressed down to the brown paper; when set the bung can be gently tapped out and the thin skin of cement at the base removed.

While the cement is still moist the first layer of pieces of walling or paving stone, which should be moistened with water before use, is now pressed into the cement, making sure that the long edge of the

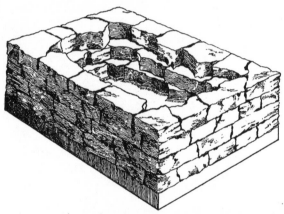

FIG. 2. *A trough made with walling or paving stone*

stone is next to the face of the box. Then another half inch of cement is added and another layer of walling stone, bonding the stone as in Fig. 2 and continuing until the height required is reached. The last layer is best laid with a spirit level so that the resultant trough is level on all sides. The overall depth is a matter of taste, but where possible this should be as deep as practicable for all rock and alpine plants require a good depth of soil as they are deep rooting plants. An added attraction in this method of building is that at odd intervals a piece of stone may be omitted, thus allowing space on the sides of the finished article for planting alpines such as ramondas, haberleas, lewisias, dianthus, etc., which never look so well as when planted on their sides against a rock face.

The completed trough should be covered with wet sacks to protect it from the harmful effects of drying winds and hot sunshine. Never attempt to build in frosty weather unless complete protection can be given. After three days the wood framework should be very carefully removed, taking care not to disturb the trough, and the cement joins should be gently roughed up with a long, pointed nail. Re-cover with damp sacks for a further week, by which time the cement will have set completely.

Using Paving Stone. The second method is to obtain some large pieces of natural paving stone between ½ and 1 inch in thickness, as near rectangular as possible, although complete accuracy is not necessary. The wooden framework as used for constructing the previous trough is utilized (see Fig. 1). Adopting the same method as before, including provision for a drainage hole, a concrete base should be laid over brown paper; it is not necessary for this to be as thick as before, 1 inch will be sufficient, for small pieces of paving stone can be embedded at the outer edges so that they touch the side of the wooden framework (see Fig. 1). While the base is still wet the rectangular pieces should be inserted on their broad ends against the side of the frame and the corners cemented with a deep fillet to ensure a strong join. When this has been completed two wooden battens cut to size should be inserted, one lengthwise and the other across and wedged, thus keeping the stone sides at right angles to the base until the cement has set. Cover the whole with damp sacking and do not touch for nine days, after which the wooden support can be removed.

Using Cement Only. The third and last method of construction is to use a cement mix only. For this two wood frames are needed (see Fig. 3), the inner one being from 2 to 3 inches smaller all round according to the size of the trough. As when using walling stone no base is required, just the brown paper. The inner framework should be constructed as in Fig. 3 to facilitate removal after the trough has set. The cement mix for this type should consist of 2 parts of coarse sand, 1 part of horticultural granulated peat, and 1 part of cement. I have found that the part of peat not only retains some of the moisture, but the plants seem to like it. The whole should be well mixed and moistened with enough water to form a pliable but not stodgy mix. As in the former methods first lay the outer framework on the brown paper and then put in enough of the mix to form the base, not forgetting the drainage hole. While still moist the inner framework should be laid gently on the base and the gap between this and the outer walls should be filled with the mixture, using a little at a time and well tamping down each layer with a wooden block. A little damp sand should be pushed into the corners of the wooden framework as the work proceeds so that when the framework is removed and the sand brushed away the edges of the finished trough will be irregular, giving it a more natural appearance. When level with the top of the outer frame the surface can be left fairly rough to match the sides.

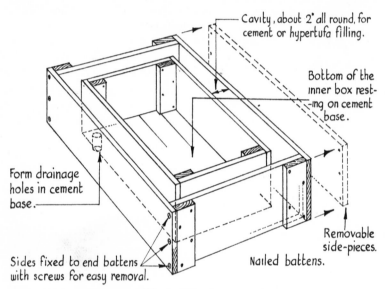

FIG. 3. *Wood mould for cement trough*

After covering with wet sacks for three days carefully remove the outer framework only, gently rough up the sides and, if necessary, fill up the gaps which may have occurred in the cement. Do not attempt to remove the inner framework for at least another week for it is essential that the trough should have set firmly before being disturbed.

Fig. 4 shows an alternative method of making a trough by building it up by hand, using a wooden former on a piece of stiff brown paper. The mixture should be firmer than that used in the previous method so that when applied it retains the shape into which it is moulded. The diagram is self-explanatory and the size of former required should suit the gardener who is constructing it.

Round Stone Troughs. The small rounded stone troughs which are so attractive can also be constructed artificially. These are quite easily made by utilizing old oyster barrels, if available, or other containers of a similar construction. The outside frame is made from a full barrel sawn off about halfway down according to the depth

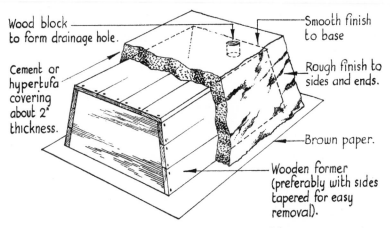

Wood block to form drainage hole.

Cement or hypertufa covering about 2" thickness.

Smooth finish to base

Rough finish to sides and ends.

Brown paper.

Wooden former (preferably with sides tapered for easy removal).

FIG. 4. *Moulding a trough over a wood former*

required, while for the inside, what is known as a half barrel is used (Fig. 5). The cement mix is the same as in all the foregoing rectangular troughs.

Very often the natural finish does not meet with favour in everybody's eyes, being too smooth to look like the real thing. There is a

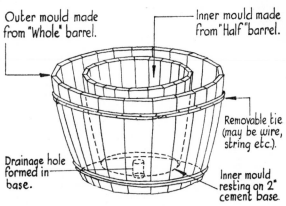

Outer mould made from "Whole" barrel.

Inner mould made from "Half" barrel.

Removable tie (may be wire, string etc.).

Drainage hole formed in base.

Inner mould resting on 2" cement base.

FIG. 5. *Mould for circular trough*

way by which this can be overcome and the result normally pleases most people. A mixture of equal parts of sand and cement, with sufficient water to bring it to the consistency of thick paint is applied with a stiff brush over the whole of the outside of the trough. No attempt must be made to provide a smooth finish, the mix should be literally slapped on. As soon as this has been applied some coarse sharp sand should be thrown on to the wet sides and left to dry. By using the various coloured sands which are obtainable different results may be obtained, or a little of the colour powders can be mixed with the cement to provide the necessary tint. These can be obtained in ochre, burnt sienna or deep green and must be used sparingly.

Washing Out Before Use. Before use all troughs, whether made of natural stone walling or paving, or those constructed of cement mixes, must be well washed out with a strong solution of water and permanganate of potash, roughly $\frac{1}{2}$ oz. of crystals to 3 gallons of water, after temporarily stopping up the drainage hole. Leave the solution in the trough for 24 hours and afterwards lightly scrub the inside with a stiff brush.

Supporting Pillars. The pillars on which to rest the troughs after completion should, where natural stone is used, be of the same material. This is best roughly hewn if obtainable and the size must be in relation to the weight they have to support. Only a rough idea can be given of sizes but the following can be used as a guide. If two pillars are to be used these will be sufficient for a trough up to 3 feet in length, and they should be the same width as the trough and not less than 4 inches in thickness. Any trough longer than 3 feet must have a central pillar as well. The pillars are best concreted into the ground to a depth of 6 inches to ensure complete rigidity. Naturally, a level must be used so that when the trough is placed on the supports it is not out of true.

For the troughs constructed of walling or paving stone the pillars can be built up on the site and, unless the pieces used are long, four pillars, one at each corner, will be a more practical proposition, being much easier to construct. The same cement mix as used for constructing the cement trough is ideal and the walling stone is bonded as if bricks were being used.

For the cement troughs the pillars can be made by constructing a framework of wood. The length of the sides should be the final height required plus the 6 inches which has to be cemented into the ground. The width is that of the trough, or, if four pillars, one at each corner, are to be used, these should be not less than 9 inches wide and 4½ inches in depth. This, as before, is laid on a piece of brown paper and the cement mix as used for the trough placed in it and well tamped down. These pillars can be reinforced, after placing about half the cement mix in the framework, by laying old chicken wire or iron pipes on top and then adding the rest of the cement up to the edge of the framework and levelling it off.

Troughs for Indoors. Although the troughs for outside use can be of any size to suit one's own surroundings, there is a considerable saving if those which are to be taken indoors for short periods either during the winter months or in early spring are made of uniform size. A good size is 18 inches by 9 inches by 6 inches deep, all outside measurements. The thickness of the base and sides need not exceed 1 inch and, by using one wooden frame, over a period a good collection of these small troughs can be built up.

Artificial Weathering. The great drawback of artificially constructed troughs is that unless treated they look home-made and too new, taking a few years to weather if Nature is left to apply her own methods. Fortunately it is possible to speed up the process of weathering and the following are three ways of accomplishing this.

First a mixture of cow manure and soot can be brushed over the whole surface. If this is too messy or the manure is not available locally the second method is quite easy to apply. All that is necessary is to apply plain milk with a spray. Lastly, a solution of water in which oatmeal has been sieved can also be sprayed on.

SCREE BEDS

When one has progressed beyond the stage of growing the easy types of rock plants, which unfortunately often require more space than can be spared in a small garden, the need arises for a special type of garden in which the choicer rock plants can be cultivated. Troughs and sinks are often utilised for this purpose, but sometimes they are difficult to obtain or do not fit in with the planting scene. In this case scree beds come into their own. To digress for a moment or two, the price of land in most areas today is at an almost prohibitive level; consequently, the large garden of yesterday even in rural areas is becoming more and more of a rarity and the normal garden of today is but a shadow of its former self. Modern architecture, too, has a tendency to be box-like or square in outline and nothing looks more unnatural in these circumstances than even a small rock garden, which requires a setting in a garden of reasonable dimensions if it is not to look out of place. Scree beds, however, are ideally suited for small gardens of the type we are now considering for they associate well with modern architecture.

Another point is that there are a number of rock plants from high altitudes which are not easy to grow in cultivation, or at least present some difficulty, due often to the fact that the environment of their natural habitat is entirely different to that offered when the plants are brought into cultivation at lower altitudes. If grown in conjunction with the easy species and varieties, conditions are such that they are soon crowded out by the more vigorous plants.

Drainage. The scree bed also provides the quick drainage that is essential for the well-being of these high altitude plants. In nature, the natural screes are found at the bases of rock formations where fragments of eroded stone have deposited themselves over a long period of time. This material combines with all the available decomposed vegetation to form detritus which thus becomes stable enough to sustain a low-growing vegetation. Once this has evolved—over many centuries—the resultant plant growth not only helps to bind the detritus but also provides sufficient nutriment by sustaining itself on its own dying vegetation. Herein lies the clue to the plant's requirements in cultivation. It is not possible to simulate Nature when making artificial scree beds, but it is of paramount importance to ensure that the drainage is perfect when constructing these beds for growing the more delicate rock plants.

Siting A Scree Bed. The construction of a scree bed is quite within the powers of the ordinary handyman and presents no great difficulty, but it should be borne in mind that it must be built well clear of any surrounding trees or dense shade of nearby buildings. Apart from this stipulation, the actual aspect is not important as there is a great variety of suitable plants that will grow in sun or semi-shade. There are a number of positions in which the bed can be built, for instance as an edging to a lawn or flower border or on a terrace.

Construction. Basically the scree bed consists of a shell in the form of a box-like structure and can be of any length to suit the site where it is to be built. The actual width will naturally depend on the available space but to be really effective should not be less than 21 inches across. The outer casing of the scree bed can be built from several types of materials; for instance natural walling stone or broken paving slabs, which are cheaper and easily obtainable from local council yards—the natural stone is expensive unless there is a source of supply locally—or manufactured concrete slabs that can be bought in a variety of shapes and sizes. For cheapness the broken paving slabs are useful as these come in a uniform thickness of 2 inches and are quite easy to lay with the aid of a spirit level, producing a neat, worthwhile job. Size is of no importance, but the slabs should not be too wide for as much space as possible is needed between the two walls for planting.

If the beds are to be built as an edging to a lawn or flower border it will be necessary to provide a firm base, consisting of a fillet of cement and ballast in the proportion of 1 part cement to 4 parts ballast (bulk, not weight), laid 3 inches deep along the sides and ends of the site. Should the scree bed be beside a lawn, the base must project about 4 inches beyond the bed to allow the use of a lawn mower right to the edge of the grass, thus saving unnecessary work in having to trim the last few inches of the lawn by hand. The slabs or natural stone are best laid in a cement mix of 3 parts builder's or soft sand to 1 part cement with the rough or broken edges facing the front of the bed. Use a spirit level to ensure that the courses of slabs are horizontal, and lay subsequent layers until the desired height is reached. The height is of some importance and will depend on what the basal medium is. On a concrete base such as one finds on a terrace the minimum should be about 12 inches or five courses of slabs and cement; this will allow enough depth for the drainage and compost. When constructing the scree bed drainage holes must be left at intervals along the base of the whole length of the structure, the gaps having pieces of perforated zinc cemented across them to prevent ingress by snails, slugs, woodlice and other pests.

On heavy clay soils the height of 12 inches is also a minimum height, for the base soil must not be used as a drainage base, otherwise after heavy or prolonged rainfall this will act as a sump with disastrous results to the plants. On walls built in this type of soil ample drainage holes must be left in the first course of stone or paving slabs, and the same precautions regarding pests taken. On light loams or sandy soils the minimum can be cut to 6 inches or about three courses of slabs for the soil base with the addition of broken rubble or other similar coarse material to provide the drainage.

The method of filling and planting these scree beds, whatever the length or depth, is as for troughs and sinks, and details will be found in Chapter Two. Naturally, the ratio of drainage to compost, depending on the depth of the beds, remains the same.

THE SCREE FRAME

The scree frame and 'billiard table' are generally neglected in books dealing with the cultivation of alpines; consequently they are almost unknown outside the gardens of specialists, yet for cultivating rock plants they can provide almost ideal conditions. The more delicate, rare and difficult plants can be grown to perfection in the former, while the latter is suitable for dwarf ericaceous plants. With the use of suitable stone perfect landscapes in miniature can be formed and enhanced with suitable plants.

FIG. 6. *The scree frame, or trough*

The best site for a scree frame is away from the informal garden and it should have a paved surround so that it can be reached on all sides during bad weather. A sunny, open position is necessary, not one overhung with trees, for rain dripping from branches can do untold damage to the plants. There is no reason why it should not be sited on a terrace adjacent to the house, but this would be a matter of personal choice.

The size of the frame depends, naturally, on the space available but the ideal is about 10 feet by 5 feet by 2½ feet high, and it can be constructed of walling stone or bricks. Frost-resisting bricks should be used, or breeze blocks which are cheaper and for which I have a personal preference. Breeze blocks are covered after construction with a rendering of cement. Both the walling stone and breeze blocks lend themselves to vertical planting; all that is necessary in the former is to leave out an occasional piece of stone when building, and in the latter small holes to take the plants can easily be made with a sharp stone chisel before rendering is applied (see Fig. 6). I use no protection in this type of frame, it is open to all that our climate can provide and the annual casualties are less than one per cent. It is possible to obtain framework of either metal or wood to cover this type of frame to provide protection where plants that flower early in the year—especially the early crocus species, *Ranunculus calandrinioides* and some of the Kabschia saxifrages—are grown. The lights can be of glass or glass substitute, which is much lighter and can be obtained in various sizes with the edges already bound.

THE 'BILLIARD TABLE'

The 'billiard table' (Fig. 7), has proved its worth in growing the rarer dwarf rhododendrons and other small ericaceous plants and from personal experience these plants never look so happy as when grown under these conditions. The table is best sited in a westerly position, that is where the sun falls on it during the late afternoon, but if this is not possible other positions can be chosen, except that the table should not face east, but the need for watering will be greater in these situations. The easterly position is avoided for the reason that these plants resent the early morning sun and cold winds, especially after cold nights; while making their new growth they are very susceptible to injury during these conditions.

There are two methods of construction. The first is as for the scree frame, the only difference being that the soil mixture used is not the same, but this is dealt with in Chapter Two (p. 36). The second method of construction is to use old railway sleepers built to a height of 3 feet and joined at each end by nailing them securely together. There is no need to use any paint or preservative for the sleepers have been steeped in creosote when first cut for their original purpose and by the time that they are discarded fumes which are normally dangerous to plant life will no longer be present.

FIG. 7. *A 'billiard table'*

PEAT BEDS

The main reason for using this type of bed in a small garden is that members of the *Ericaceae* and kindred families can be grown under almost ideal conditions. If cultivated with the larger species and varieties, such as some of the alpine rhododendrons for example, they tend to be overshadowed, whereas if suitable positions can be provided separately in specially prepared peat beds one can enjoy the delicate individual beauty of these exquisite miniatures. This type of bed is essential should the natural soil of the garden have a high lime content. Here again, with ever-increasing numbers of houses to the acre being built, with the resultant loss of natural light, this form of gardening can present the answer to these conditions. A point to bear in mind is that almost without exception air, humidity and sunshine are closely bound up in the successful cultivation of these plants—the higher the amount of moisture in the atmosphere the greater the tolerance of sun, and vice versa. Simply, it means that in hot, dry gardens more shade is needed than in moister ones. From the geographical viewpoint shade is needed in the South,

East Anglia and the Midlands, whereas in the extreme West Country and the North a greater degree of sun is required. Bearing this in mind the bed can be sited on its own, at the base of a tree or the shady side of a hedge or clump of shrubs.

Whatever site is chosen, the area should be marked out first of all in any desired shape to suit the situation, the more informal the better. On a neutral or acid medium the top 6 inches must be well dug, cleaned of all roots, especially those from trees, which should be cut off and removed, and plenty of decayed leafmould (in preference to peat) mixed in at the same time. The leafmould will provide nourishment, which peat will not, being generally sterile and inert. A small but important point to remember is that the leafmould must come from a neutral source. Where the natural soil is limy the ground is best left firm and a 3-inch layer of really rough bracken peat laid on the surface. The more acid this medium is the better. If watered with Sequestrene, a product based on an iron chelate with magnesium and manganese added and marketed to correct iron deficiency in alkaline soils, this will allow one to grow the lime-hating plants. It will be found necessary to repeat the dosage as advised at infrequent intervals.

To make the peat bed, peat blocks are used to retain the soil and these may be purchased from a variety of sources. Their size is not important, provided they are uniform, although blocks 12 × 6 inches and 4 inches deep are ideal. It is essential that the blocks should be moist before building is commenced for once they are in position it will be found almost impossible to make them absorb sufficient water. If for some reason or other they are dry it will be necessary to soak them in water for at least 24 hours before use. This is best carried out by immersing the blocks in a tank or some other container filled with water. It is almost certain that pieces of rock or other material will be needed to submerge the blocks during this process. Watering with a hose or watering-can is hopeless as the water runs off the peat blocks before they are able to absorb any of it.

Construction. The method of building the wall is the same as laying a dry wall, each layer of peat blocks being bonded; these should have a slight inward tilt as each layer is laid. As building takes place a soil mixture comprising 4 parts of leafmould, 1 part fibrous neutral loam and 1 part coarse sand should be used as one would mortar, working the mixture into all cracks and crevices as the wall is built and filling the body of the bed at the same time with a similar mixture. It is not necessary to build high, 12 inches will be ample. This means about three courses of peat blocks will be required if they are 4 inches deep. This height should certainly be the maximum in districts where the average rainfall is low, as there may be a tendency for the soil to dry out too rapidly in a prolonged dry spell if the wall is higher than this. In some areas birds present a problem, especially blackbirds who like nothing better than to pull a wall to pieces. It will pay to peg the blocks down by driving thin iron rods through the centre of each block; these will effectively pin down the structure and make it secure. Methods used for planting are dealt with in Chapter Two.

If for any reason it is not possible to obtain peat blocks, a good substitute, which is not only suitable but artistic too, is to build the walls of the bed with tree logs. These are most effective if not less than 4 inches in diameter and not greater than 6 inches, and curved if possible. Should only straight sections be available the ends are best cut at an angle, to enable them to fit into any required pattern. It is essential for them to be treated for freedom from rot and fungus disease with a copper-based wood preserver (on no account must one with a creosote base be used), which will act not only as a rot preventer but also as a fungicide. Two tiers will be found sufficient and when placed on top of each other nails long enough to tie them securely are driven in.

ROCK POTS

This chapter would not be complete without reference to the rock pots, both natural and artificially made, which have become so popular. The rarer plants seem to thrive and retain their dwarf, congested habit under this method of cultivation.

Tufa. This natural stone occurs in a few places in this country. It is unfortunately rather expensive to purchase, but it is not so heavy in weight, bulk for bulk, as ordinary limestone or sandstone. It is composed of calcareous deposits formed by rivers and streams and is normally rich in lime and very porous. An added advantage is that it is easy to work, and holes large enough to take plants can be made by the use of a hammer and chisel. The one disadvantage is that this stone can only be used for lime-loving plants. The pieces of tufa should be purchased as large as possible so that a variety of plants can be grown, providing a delightful picture.

Hypertufa. The first of the artificially made stones has been named Hypertufa by F. H. Fisher, a Past President of the Alpine Garden Society, who first experimented with this medium for growing rock plants. I have found that it is ideal for growing cushion plants and some of the more difficult alpines and, unlike tufa, plants which are strongly calcifuge can be safely grown in this medium.

It is easily and cheaply constructed and can be made in any size to suit one's own requirements. An irregular hole to the size needed is

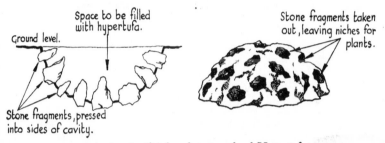

FIG. 8. *Artificial rock pot made of Hypertufa*

dug in a piece of ground and small pieces of irregularly shaped stone are pushed up to 2 inches into the sides and bottom of the ground, as many as the number of plants required (see Fig. 8). Next, a mixture is prepared consisting of 1 part of cement, and 1 of sand to 2 parts of Sorbex peat to which has been added enough water to make up a workable mix. The peat must not be used in a dry condition but should be soaked in water. The mixture should be placed carefully in the prepared hole, adding a little at a time until it is level with the ground. It is then left for six days before being carefully dug out. The pieces of stone are then removed by gently tapping them out with a hammer. Afterwards the rock is covered with damp sacks for a further five days. The piece of Hypertufa should then be soaked with water for two days when it will be ready for use.

Rock Pots of Stone. The second method of constructing artificial rocks, known as rock pots, is by using pieces of real stone, either sand or limestone, and cementing them together, forming an irregular pot.

A base made up of equal parts of cement, sand and garden peat is laid about 1 inch deep on a piece of brown paper. In the centre a small piece of broom handle is inserted for the drainage hole. Pieces of rock are placed on the cement base and joined together to form a large open pot (see Fig. 9), working the cement well into the joints. Cover the finished article with damp sacks for a day then carefully

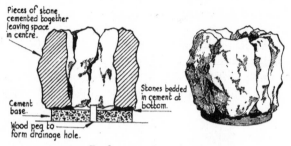

FIG. 9. *Rock pot made with natural stone*

cut away the base of the cement which is protruding round the sides of the pot. After a further period of six days the pot should be washed with water, then it will be ready for planting.

Fig. 10 shows another rock pot made from Hypertufa and fragments of natural stone and this is an ideal container for small bulbous plants, sempervivums, saxifrages of the Kabschia or Engleria types,

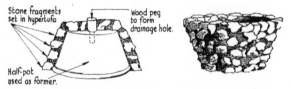

FIG. 10. *Rock pot of Hypertufa and stone fragments*

and other early flowering plants. It is very useful for bringing indoors during the flowering period in spring, being much more decorative than the ordinary flower pot. Plants seem to like this type of pot—possibly due to its partly organic composition, in the form of peat—which retains moisture much better than the clay pot.

Aethionema pulchellum (see p. 128).

Alyssum spinosum roseum (see p. 87).

Above left: *Andromeda polifolia compacta* (see p. 88).
Above right: *Arenaria tetraquetra* (see p. 90).
Below: *Cassiope tetragona* (see p. 92).

CHAPTER TWO

PREPARING THE TROUGHS

Compost Ingredients, Preparing the Composts, Troughs and Planting

WHEN the troughs or sinks have been purchased or built and suitable sites chosen, thought must be given to the soil composts, planting and placing of the rocks to complete the picture. All these operations are complementary to one another, each playing its own part in the finished landscape in miniature, and a certain amount of care in preparation is essential for success.

COMPOSTS

Unlike the open rock garden in which the soil has to be taken as found or replaced partly by alien compost, not always with successful results, troughs and sinks are under the control of the amateur who can experiment with various mixtures to suit his or her own idea as to what the plants require. At one time or another the use of many different soil mixtures has been advocated, but my own conclusions, drawn from years of experience in growing these dwarf plants, are that, bearing in mind site and position with regard to sun and shade, and the district in which the plants are to be grown, four mixtures should cover the whole range of plants.

The ingredients of the soil compost are of major importance and should be chosen with care, for the extra time and trouble taken to obtain the right materials before filling the troughs will amply repay the cultivator. It is easy enough to say that any old potting soil or soil mixture will do to fill the trough and then proceed to plant in mixtures that may not only be entirely unsuitable but even disease and pest ridden. If such mixtures are used, the trough will possibly have to be completely remade when it is found that its occupants are not thriving. This is not only a waste of time and money but also acutely disappointing. The cultivator rarely blames himself—it is invariably the nurseryman from whom the plants were purchased or the gardening book or periodical consulted which was at fault! So I will say this to all those who wish to succeed in growing these plants: the majority are extremely easy provided the growing medium is correct and clean and there is no reason why a young healthy specimen, correctly planted, should not thrive.

The materials needed are not many and I will deal with each individually, starting with those needed to prepare the four composts referred to on p. 36.

Loam. This must be of a heavy, greasy texture but not pure clay, completely interlaced with fibrous material well rotted down and completely neutral as to its lime content. Lime can always be added where this is necessary although I have found that it is rarely essential; even those plants which are supposed to demand lime to give of their best have always thrived in a neutral medium with me. A slightly more limy content can be obtained by top-dressing with limestone chippings; these will leach out a small amount of lime with rain or artificial watering. On the other hand a loam which is from a limy district is of no use if it is desired to grow members of the family *Ericaceae*, which includes rhododendron, erica, gaultheria, etc., for all these are intolerant of lime. Once a reliable source has been found, it is best, if possible, to obtain loam always from that source and not to change from one district to another.

Leafmould. The best leafmould is obtained from oak and beech leaves and it should be well rotted, crumbling and flaking when well rubbed down between the fingers. A word of caution though: leafmould from beech leaves is liable to contain lime for the beech is native on chalky soils, so here again care must be used if the plants are lime-haters.

Horticultural Peat. This is a well-known product generally sold in bales tightly compressed. When pulled out and sieved this provides the gardener with light, clean, weed- and pest-free material. A point worth noting here is that after sieving it must be well watered for it is normally extremely dry.

Sand. A really sharp sand is needed for the compost, such as Bedfordshire silver sand or Cornish silver sand. I have a preference for the latter which is made up of particles ranging in size from the dimensions of a small pea to those of a pin's head. Cornish silver sand never packs under any conditions.

Spent Hops or Peat Roughage. These are ideal for placing over the drainage material before putting the soil compost in the trough. If the hops are unobtainable the residue of the horticultural peat after sieving is just as good.

Bonemeal. A small quantity can be added to the composts after mixing. A teaspoonful to a gallon by bulk of compost is sufficient. This being a very slow-acting fertilizer it will retain its efficiency over a long period without the necessity of replenishing yearly.

PREPARING THE COMPOSTS

The majority of plants suitable for culture in troughs and sinks will do well in a compost which contains a small amount of nourishment. A rich soil will only lead to rank growth and its attendant ills, and provide a juicy meal for pests. It is essential that the mixture should be open so that any surplus moisture can easily drain away. The heavy loam with the addition of bonemeal will contain all the necessary food for a considerable period and the addition of sand, leafmould and peat keeps the compost open and well-drained. The leafmould and peat provide the necessary humus and the sand, of course, while in itself sterile, is used to help the drainage and lighten the compost.

Both the loam and leafmould should be sterilized. They can either be purchased already sterilized, or the job can be done at home. Much trouble can be avoided by cleansing the loam and leafmould before use, for by starting with a weed- and pest-free compost it will reduce labour, time and very often disappointment to a minimum. The method of sterilization is described in Chapter Three (see p. 44). It is not necessary to sterilize either the peat or sand for both should be free from weed seeds and pests when purchased. The materials, with the exception of the peat, should be rubbed down between the fingers. All the fibrous material from the loam must be retained; this can be pulled to pieces and mixed with the compost. The peat is best riddled through an $\frac{1}{8}$-inch sieve, the residue being used over the drainage. Plants seem to appreciate a mixture which, being granular in texture, does not readily pack and harden into a mass which will rapidly become impervious to moisture, a state of affairs that will soon spell disaster if all the materials are finely sieved. The roots of plants, like human beings, require a certain amount of oxygen to give of their best and the granular composition of the compost ensures that there are minute air spaces through which the air circulates freely after the water has drained away. All the composts are measured by bulk, not weight, and the ingredients must be mixed thoroughly, turning them well a number of times, slightly dampening the mixture with a fine-rosed watering can. Allow such composts to stand for a day and they will then be ready for use.

SUITABLE COMPOSTS

The four composts described below should be all that are needed to grow a mixed and varied collection of plants, and in each case I have given a rough idea of the mixture's suitability for various purposes. In the Descriptive List of Plants (pp. 87 to 127), the mixtures referred to by letter are those described below, and although it is unwise to be dogmatic over the suitability of this or that mixture, a basis must be prepared and from this experiments can be carried out as one's experience of growing alpines in troughs develops.

Compost A. Equal parts of loam, leafmould and sand.

This is a suitable mixture for plants which require a light, open, porous soil with good drainage. A good mixture for troughs in a sheltered position in half shade. All bulbs and conifers do well in this medium.

Compost B. Equal parts of loam, leafmould, peat and sand.

This is more retentive of water but is well drained and will grow all the plants mentioned in the Descriptive List as suitable for full sun and it is ideal for woodland plants in half shade.

Compost C. Four parts leafmould and one part each of loam and sand.

A soil for growing dwarf rhododendrons and other ericaceous plants in the 'billiard table' type of trough and peat beds.

Compost D. Three parts Cornish silver sand and one part flaked leafmould.

For all difficult and rare high alpines, including most of the cushion type. The trough containing this mixture is best situated in half shade.

ROCKS AND CHIPPINGS

Rocks. These are necessary to build up miniature landscapes and are obtainable quite cheaply from nurserymen who deal in rockwork. A selection of various kinds can be bought, such as the waterworn limestones, sandstones and tufa. As this material is cheap and easy to

Above left: *Crocus fleischeri* (see p. 93).
Above right: *Crocus vernus* (see p. 130).
Below: *Cyclamen europaeum* (see p. 94).

ABOVE LEFT: *Dodecatheon pauciflorum* (see p. 130).
ABOVE RIGHT: *Epigaea asiatica* (see p. 96).
BELOW LEFT: *Geranium cinereum album* (see p. 98).
BELOW RIGHT: *Hebe pimeleoides* (see p. 99).

procure most sundriesmen are only too glad to get rid of those small pieces which are of no use in the rock garden. Artificial stones are unnecessary as well as undesirable.

Chippings. These are used for the final top-dressing and are obtainable generally as limestone or granite and should be purchased in sizes ranging from $\frac{1}{2}$ inch to $\frac{1}{4}$ inch.

PREPARING THE TROUGHS

Natural and artificial troughs must first of all be cleansed by washing them out with a strong solution of permanganate of potash, placing a cork stopper in the drainage hole and then with a stiff broom or brush well scrubbing the sides and base. Afterwards, a good rinse with clear water will complete the cleaning.

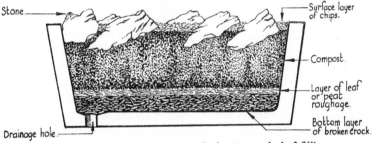

Stone — — — Surface layer of chips.

— Compost.

— Layer of leaf or peat roughage.

— Bottom layer of broken crock.

Drainage hole —

FIG. II. *Sectional view of trough showing method of filling*

Ensuring Adequate Drainage. A piece of perforated zinc should be placed over the vent at the base of the trough. This serves a double purpose, for it allows all surplus water to drain away and denies access to the trough to such pests as woodlice and slugs. Next, 2 inches of drainage material is placed in the trough. This can consist of broken pots, cleaned clinker, or broken bricks. I have a preference for bricks as I find that although they allow the rapid passage of water a certain amount is retained for use by the roots of the plants. Over the drainage material is placed a fine layer of roughage, either the residue of peat or leafmould after sieving, or spent hops, if obtainable. Its function is primarily to prevent the compost from filtering down into the drainage and blocking it.

Filling. The appropriate compost is then placed on top of the roughage and the trough filled to the top, after which it should be firmed, then well watered and left for a day or two to settle. A further firming should then be made and any shrinkage made good, when the trough will be ready for planting (see Fig. 11).

Planting. Naturally I cannot give details of what to plant but only general instructions on how to plant. The choice of plants for each trough must depend on the personal likes and dislikes of the grower, but study of the list of plants and the illustrations of troughs complete with their occupants will do much to eliminate mistakes such as planting quick-growing plants with slow, sun-lovers with shade-lovers (unless suitable shade can be given with the aid of stone), lime-loving plants in an acid mixture, or acid-loving plants in a limy medium.

The majority of rock plants are sold in pots and can, with few exceptions, be planted at all times of the year except, perhaps, in mid-winter and during frosty periods. The best time is in early spring for it is at this period that root growth is starting once more and the plants quickly become re-established in their new home.

There are two methods of planting. I will describe first what I will call the orthodox way, for want of a better term. Take the pot with its occupant, remove any chippings from the surface of the pot, place the second and third fingers of the right hand under the foliage round the neck of the plant if it comes from a central rootstock, turn the pot upside down and with the wooden handle of a trowel give the rim a sharp tap to loosen the plant; the pot can then be lifted clear. Gently remove the drainage material and insert the plant into its position in the trough, in a hole already made large enough to take the plant without pushing or forcing it. Then make the compost firm round the plant and settle it in its new home by applying slight pressure with the fingers, not thumbs, of both hands. The neck of the plant must be kept clear of any soil for at least $\frac{1}{2}$ inch, and, after a good watering in, a top-dressing of the appropriate chippings will complete the planting. There is one great drawback with this method and that is nurserymen naturally have to make a saleable plant in as short a period as possible so they invariably use a richer compost than is desirable or necessary for this purpose. Sometimes it is found that after planting the specimen goes ahead for a few months and then stagnates, begins to go back and finally passes away. When the corpse is lifted it is noticed that the roots instead of going into the new compost have just worked themselves into a hard ball in the old soil and there remained until the old compost has literally disappeared.

In the other method, and this is the one I always use, all the compost in which the plant is growing is either shaken or washed off. The roots are then carefully spread out in the new soil and made firm after working in the compost at the roots without causing them damage. A good watering is then given, the plant is shaded for a few days and overhead syringing with water is carried out in the evenings until it has re-established itself. For the high alpine, rare and difficult cushion plants to be grown in the scree mixture D and for any plant which has become pot-bound this method is essential; the removal of all old soil and gentle teasing out of the roots is necessary for any chance of success. When this method is adopted additional care is needed at planting time, and as the plants should be in active growth this naturally restricts the period when it can be utilized.

I should like to give a word of advice here to beginners; always use small, well-grown plants and do not plant large specimens for the chance of re-establishing them successfully decreases as the size of the plant increases.

For planting in cracks or crevices of tufa or natural stone it is essential that small rooted cuttings are used so that the roots can be safely and gently worked into the cracks. A small amount of compost A, to which has been added the grit of the tufa or natural stone from the hole or crevice, is then placed round the roots and neck of the plant and carefully watered in until the roots are completely under the cushion or rosette of the plant and are not in direct contact with any of the compost. Until re-established the same care is given as advocated for scree plants.

Placing Rocks. The small pieces of rock should be used either for artistic effect or utilitarian purpose. From the artistic viewpoint your imagination must be brought into play. I would just give a little piece of advice; most natural stone has distinctive strata and when using it it is better that the stone is laid so that the strata are uniform as they would be found in Nature (see Fig. 12). It is a fallacy to state, as do the majority of gardening books giving advice on this subject, that at least two-thirds of the stone should be buried, pointing to the natural outcrops in the wilds as evidence of this. It would be much nearer the truth to say that nine hundred and ninety-nine thousandths should be buried for this is nearer the ratio in a natural outcrop. If the stones are placed so that their broadest base is laid just below the surface of the soil and the compost is then well firmed around them, the roots of the plants will find ideal conditions under their bases.

The value of stone for utilitarian purposes is that it can be built up
to provide homes for choice and delicate plants which often thrive

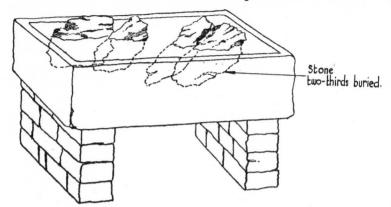

Stone
two-thirds buried.

FIG. 12. *Trough, showing natural use of stone*

much better when planted in this manner (see Fig. 13). The need for
a much quicker draining medium in our moisture-laden atmosphere
than is required by the plants in their natural habitat is met by constructing a home for them above the level of the trough. Naturally,

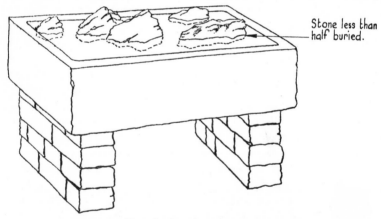

Stone less than
half buried.

FIG. 13. *Trough, showing utilitarian use of stone*

care is essential, especially during the first year after planting or if
the weather is exceptionally dry and windy, until the roots have gone
down into the main body of the soil in the trough, where all the necessary moisture for their requirements is to be found.

Top-dressing. All planting in any single trough should be completed at one time, as far as it is practicable; then after the rocks have been placed in position a top-dressing of the appropriate chippings, limestone or granite, can be added to complete the picture.

Peat Beds and 'Billiard Tables'. For the peat beds and the 'billiard table' type of garden the same planting methods are employed, but here stone is used for the purpose of providing shade or wind protection for the choice plants, and instead of chippings a top-dressing of not less than an inch of rough, moist peat is desirable, this being renewed annually before the weather becomes too dry in late spring. A further top-dressing of the same material can also be given in late autumn, especially if any of the plants being grown are suspect as to hardiness.

All other troughs, sinks, scree beds and scree frames should be top-dressed in early spring with $\frac{1}{2}$ inch of the same compost as that which is being used for filling the particular trough, sink or scree frame in question, and this must be well watered in.

Watering. No hard and fast rules can be laid down with regard to watering, important as this factor is when growing rock plants in troughs. Different methods apply in different climatic situations. For example, less water will be required by plants growing in the moister atmosphere of the North than in the South, just as less will be required in gardens in the West compared with those in the East of the country.

During the first year after planting care must be taken to see that the plants do not suffer from lack of water until they have become well-established. My experience, for what it is worth, and remembering that the average annual rainfall in West Kent (where I live) is approximately 24 inches, is that from the time growth starts in early spring until late September overwatering is unlikely. It should not be necessary to water from October until the following spring unless a really dry period is experienced.

CHAPTER THREE

PROPAGATION

Seed, Division, Cuttings, Frames for Cuttings, their Construction and Management

A knowledge of propagating alpine plants is essential for gardeners who wish to increase their stock. Many of these plants are expensive to buy and often not easy to procure at any price. This is understandable when it is realized that, being small even when fully grown, many rock plants can only give a limited number of cuttings; in fact, where every shoot is carrying flower these are impossible to obtain, and often seed is only sparsely set. As with all things where the demand exceeds the supply the cost is generally high.

There are five methods of reproduction, namely, seed, cuttings, layering, division and grafting, but we need only deal with seed, cuttings and division. Layering in a number of instances is a good method but it is not recommended as it invariably entails spoiling the look of the trough and disturbing the other occupants of the trough for a period of twelve months or so while the shoots to be layered are pegged into a sandy mixture. Grafting must be avoided like the plague, for plants which are increased by this method with very few exceptions lose all their dwarf characteristics in a short space of time and the balance of the trough is soon upset.

SEED

Where good seed is procurable and breeds true, this, Nature's method of reproducing the species, should be used wherever possible. A plant raised from seed is a new entity and unlike a cutting is less liable to disease, but unfortunately some genera, such as aquilegia, lewisia, etc., cannot be relied upon to breed true, but cross with all and sundry species of the same genus that are being grown in the vicinity. True, there is always the possibility of a new hybrid or even an outstanding colour form appearing and this is a further inducement to raise plants from seed.

The Viability of Seed. Seed must be sown as soon as it is ripe where there is any doubt as to its viability. Many seeds have a very short life and those of some genera such as *Anemone* and *Primula*, especially the Asiatic primulas, should be sown at once to obtain good results. Also, if there is delay in sowing, germination may sometimes not take place for a period which may extend into three years. Gentians are notoriously slow germinators, and if the seed is not sown when ripe there is invariably a delay of a year before it germinates. No seed which has not sprouted should be thrown away for at least two years. The pans should be placed in a cool, north-facing position and kept moist, exposing them to all available snow and frost which will very often have the effect of inducing the seed to germinate.

Generally, the smaller the seed the shorter the time it will remain viable. Seed of the more common and less difficult plants is best sown at the end of February. This will allow a good six months' growth during the spring and summer, resulting in nice sturdy specimens ready for planting out in early September.

John Innes Seed Compost. For this type of seed the John Innes Seed Compost is very suitable and efficient. It can be purchased already mixed from all good nursery or garden sundriesmen, but the compost can be readily mixed at home at a great saving, especially if a large amount is required. All the following ingredients are by bulk not weight, and should be well mixed together dry, storing for a day or so before use: 2 parts of heavy loam from well-rotted, stacked turves (this loam should be obtained from a reliable source), 1 part sieved leafmould or horticultural peat and 1 part Cornish sand. The loam must be sterilized to rid it of harmful weed seeds and pests, and then be rubbed down between the fingers until it is granular in texture, retaining all the fibrous material which if too large for inclusion may be cut up with a pair of scissors. On no account must it be sieved. One-and-a-half ounces of superphosphate of lime and $\frac{3}{4}$ oz. of chalk is added to each bushel of compost. If the seed to be sown belongs to a genus which abhors lime the chalk must be omitted.

Other Seed Composts. For the rarer and more difficult sun-loving plants which require care and attention to bring them to maturity the following is a good compost:

Equal parts of heavy fibrous sterilized loam and leafmould, sieved through a $\frac{1}{16}$-inch sieve, to two parts of coarse sand.

Shade-loving dwarf rhododendrons and other ericaceous plants are best suited to an open spongy compost consisting of equal parts of leafmould, peat and coarse sand.

It is absolutely essential that all the materials, including the seed pans, should be scrupulously clean and the compost must be sterilized.

Seed Pans. Pans are used in preference to boxes for raising seed for three reasons. They will not rot, and it may be necessary to keep them for a period of years before the seed germinates, and woodlice are not attracted to the pans as much as they are to the wooden boxes. Lastly, I am of the opinion that if porous pans are used for raising plants from seed, it is possible to maintain the seed compost at a more uniform temperature and moisture content.

Sterilizing Materials. There are a number of good commercial sterilizing units on the market today and, provided the maker's recommendations are carried out, all are extremely efficient and reliable. If only a small amount of seed raising is to be attempted, necessitating the minimum amount of materials, the answer is, possibly, to buy the ingredients already sterilized, but the following method is ideal for those possessing an electric oven. It is only necessary to sterilize the loam and leafmould to be used, for the horticultural peat is normally pest and weed free. The leafmould and loam are sterilized separately—each must be moist but not wet throughout. An average-sized electric oven can accommodate up to a gallon in bulk of each material which should be placed in a clean piece of dry sacking, the four corners tied together with string and suspended from a grid placed high in the oven. After closing the door the current is switched on and a careful watch kept until the thermometer on the outside of the oven reaches 177°C (350°F), then the power is turned off and the material being sterilized is allowed to remain for a further thirty-five minutes. Should an oven without an outside thermometer be used a thermometer of the type used for jam-making can be placed inside, but more care will be needed to see that the temperature does not exceed 177°C. As a rough guide it will take between fifteen and twenty minutes to reach this heat. The loam or leafmould is then taken into the open air or the potting shed, the corners of the sacking are undone and the sterilized material is spread out to cool. After a few hours it will be ready for use. A small but important point to remember is that one should only prepare sufficient compost to meet one's current needs for I have found the useful life of the prepared mixture to be no greater than two months.

Cleaning Pans. The pans and crocking material to be used must be well cleaned by scrubbing them with hot soapy water or a solution

Helichrysum sibthorpii (see p. 131).

Heloniopsis orientalis var. *yakusimensis* (see p. 131).

Iberis jordanii (see p. 101).

Jasminum parkeri (see p. 101).

containing one of the many detergents in use today, sterilizing them afterwards by plunging them into a strong solution of permanganate of potash. The pans must be allowed to dry out but not to such an extent that when the compost is added the pan will absorb all its moisture. On the other hand, if the pan is used damp the soil will adhere to the sides so that when the seedlings are turned out there will be a considerable loss of the small fibrous roots to the detriment of the seedlings. If new pans are used these must be soaked for at least twenty-four hours before use so that the intense dryness due to their being kiln-fired is removed. Here, again, the pans must be dried off before use.

Preparing the Pans. The method of preparing the pan for seedlings is quite simple but like all simple things this does not mean care is not required. First place a crock or a piece of perforated zinc over the vent or vents in the pan. I have a preference for zinc as by using it pests such as slugs or woodlice are prevented from entering through the base. An inch of drainage material, broken crocks or chippings, is then placed over the zinc or crock, and a covering of roughage (such as the residue of leafmould after being sifted) is next placed on top of the crocks. Just enough is used to cover the crocks completely so that the compost will not be able to work down and block the drainage. Finally the requisite compost is added to within an inch of the top of the pan and made firm; a round disk of wood slightly smaller than the smallest seed pan is ideal for this purpose. Good pressure should be applied, for a firm surface, especially round the sides of the pan, is essential. When completed the pan must be placed in a container with 2 inches of water and allowed to remain until the surface of the compost darkens, when it should be removed and stood on one side to allow any excess water to drain away.

Sowing Seed. The seed of rock plants can vary in size from a pin's head to almost dust and in relation to its size different methods of sowing are needed. A good maxim to follow is that where the seed is large enough a sowing depth equal to the width of the seed is about right. Very fine seed need only be sprinkled on the surface over a layer of coarse sand, no further treatment or coverage being required. Large seeds should, where practicable, be sown individually, allowing enough space between each seed for the young seedlings to develop without undue crowding. In this way strong, sturdy plants are produced, easily removed for potting up with a minimum of root disturbance. To facilitate the sowing of very fine seed evenly and not too thickly it should be mixed with 4 parts of silver sand to 1 of seed and broadcast lightly over the surface of the prepared pan. A large sugar sifter or one of the cardboard canisters in which pepper, curry powder, etc. are sold is ideal for distributing the mixture of sand and seed evenly. A small but important point, for it can mean the difference between success and failure, is that the sand used must be dry.

Seeds of dwarf rhododendrons, most other ericaceous, and many woodland plants are best sown direct on to a fine layer of sphagnum moss which has been laid on top of the compost and made firm. After this no further covering is needed.

Treatment after Sowing. The seed pans when sown should be placed in a cool north-facing spot outdoors or in a cold frame in a similar position, and be covered either with a sheet of slate or asbestos and kept moist. Watering must be carried out by immersing the pans in a tank or similar container holding 2 inches of water and allowing them to remain in this until the surface of the compost darkens. On no account should water be applied overhead for not only will this mean that the seeds are liable to be washed into a corner of the pan, but the surface of the pan quickly becomes a breeding place for lichen, liverwort, etc., the spores of which are easily carried by watering from a can. In districts where liverwort is rife this pest can destroy seedlings or completely stop germination. A watch should be kept for any appearance of this or lichen and they must be removed at once, using a fine needle and carefully lifting them from the surface of the compost without undue disturbance. Some experts advise the turning of the coverings every day but I have never found this to be necessary. Once the seed has germinated, however, the covers must be removed immediately.

Potting on. Germination may be uneven but all seedlings must be removed and potted on as soon as they have formed their first true leaves. For the gardener who is attempting his first raising of plants from seed I would like to explain that the first pair of leaves which appear through the surface of the soil are known as cotyledons and are invariably spoon-shaped, with the exception of corms, bulbs, tubers and grasses which produce some form of a lance-shaped leaf. The next pair of leaves are the true leaves which are identical with those of the parent plant and show characteristics of the genus from which the seed has come.

When removing the seedlings from the seed pan great care is essential for more plants are lost during this stage than possibly at any other time of their lives. Damage to the roots must be avoided, especially where the plant forms a tap root, for if this is broken invariably a deformed, weakly plant is the result, even if the seedling survives the injury.

First the pan should be dipped in a tank and the compost well moistened, then it will be possible to lift out the young seedling without injury to its roots. A very handy tool for this purpose can be made from a piece of hardwood, oak, teak, etc., shaped like a wedge at one end and with a notch cut in the other, roughly 6 inches in length by ⅜ inch wide. With this tool it is possible to lift the delicate seedlings from the pan without causing damage or bruising, as the cotyledons form a collar which holds the seedling upright ready to be placed in its new pot.

Small 'thumbs' or 2-inch pots should be used for the first potting and the soil mixture, which is placed over good drainage, should be the appropriate seed compost plus an extra part of heavy loam. The compost must be firmed round the seedling but excess pressure near the neck of the plant must be avoided for damage at this point will cause the collapse of the seedling. A light top-dressing of small chips will protect the plant from collar rot, and will keep the surface of the soil from drying and caking. The pots are best placed in a closed frame in a shady place for a few days until root action is apparent. This is indicated by the seedling growing away strongly, when air must be increasingly given, until after a week the lights may be removed. From this potting the young plants may be placed in their final quarters, but if this is not practicable, by the time they have filled their pots with roots they must be repotted into pots a size larger. It is in this early stage of their life that the young plants must be grown on without a check if they are to give of their best.

DIVISION

A large number of rock plants, especially the easier species and varieties, can be increased by division; in fact, possibly the only plants which cannot be increased successfully in this way are those which form a tap root. The best time for carrying out the operation is in early spring, that is late March till the end of May, according to the district in which the plants are growing; in the north and east of this country the later date is more suitable, whereas in southern and western districts the early to middle dates are ideal. The plant to be divided should have all the soil removed from its roots by washing in clean water and then it should be pulled into small pieces, each section having a number of roots attached. These pieces are then potted up singly in a mixture of equal parts leafmould, loam and coarse sand and are placed in a cool, closed, shady frame until they have become established, when air should be admitted and the plants hardened off ready for planting in their permanent quarters. No flower bud should be allowed to remain on the plant as all its energy must be concentrated on root formation while it is re-establishing itself.

Difficult, rare or delicate plants which often only have a few wiry roots should, after division, be treated as cuttings and re-established in a cutting frame (described on pp. 51 to 59).

CUTTINGS

This method of increasing stock is widely used by professional nurserymen and amateurs and, in fact, in many cases, it is the only way of increasing plants. Another great advantage of this method of propagation is that unlike raising plants from seed, which can only be carried out over a limited period, by using the different forms of cuttings plus a little heat at times it is possible to increase plants at almost any period of the year. Hybrids, good colour forms and sports cannot be perpetuated in any other way although in some commercial houses grafting is carried out, thus providing a larger, more saleable specimen in a shorter space of time. This method of propagation should be avoided at all costs where dwarf rock plants suitable for troughs and sinks are required for the plant resulting from the graft will invariably be more vigorous and quicker growing than one from a cutting. As the factor determining the suitability of plants for troughs is the slow normal rate of growth it will be readily observed that any departure from this must be avoided if the scenic balance is not to be overthrown or individual plant characteristics modified. There is one important point to remember and that is that no cuttings should be taken from a flowering shoot for it is extremely doubtful if these will root.

There are five different kinds of cuttings with which I will deal—green cuttings, half-ripened cuttings, hardwood cuttings, root cuttings and leaf cuttings.

Dwarf rhododendrons, ericas and other ericaceous plants as well as a maple provide interest in the author's peat garden.

A well-established trough planting with dwarf phlox, *Oxalis adenophylla*, *Arabis bryoides*, *Lithospermum oleifolium* and *Haberlea rhodopensis*.

A trough with free-flowering specimens of the deep pink *Dianthus* Elizabeth and *Oxalis chrysantha*.

Aquilegia flabellata nana, a delightful dwarf form of a Japanese species (see p. 89).

Green Cuttings. These are cuttings taken from the new growth and are extremely soft and delicate, needing care when inserting them in the rooting compost. They are best struck in a tightly-closed frame and should not be allowed to flag. They will then root very often in a matter of days. Naturally, as in all other garden operations, much depends on the weather and the times given here are for a normal season. If the spring is early the date can be advanced a week or so, or retarded if the spring is cold and late. All dates quoted here are for the south of the country, the Midlands will need a further week's growth and the North and Scotland will need up to two weeks more. April and May are the best periods for taking green cuttings.

The cutting is prepared by using a razor blade and cutting at a node, making sure that the cut is cleanly made and any foliage carefully removed to one third of its length. Only a small batch at a time should be taken for this type of cutting quickly flags.

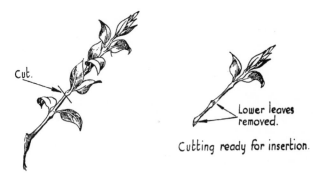

Cut.

Lower leaves removed.

Cutting ready for insertion.

Cutting before preparation.

FIG. 14. *Preparing half-ripened cuttings*

Half-ripened Cuttings. These are taken from the plant when the base of the cutting is hard but the growing tip is quite firm yet not hard. Most evergreen plants, including dwarf shrubs and conifers, can be increased by this method and the use of bottom heat will not only speed up the operation but it is often the only means of rooting certain types of plants. The ability to know just when the shoot is ready and ripe enough to take can only be gained with experience and it is recommended that cuttings be taken over a period until the propagator is able to distinguish between a good or bad cutting. A rough guide is that the shoots of the plant to be propagated should crack or break readily when bent. June and July and possibly the first two weeks of August are the best times at which to take cuttings of this nature (Fig. 14).

Hardwood Cuttings. These are taken from really ripened growth of the current year and should be hard and firm along the whole length of the shoot. They are generally taken from deciduous plants at the end of October and placed in the cutting frame where, if allowed to remain over the winter, rooting will start in spring. This type of cutting is taken by giving a side shoot a sharp downward pull so that it comes away with a heel of the old wood attached. It is now prepared for the cutting frame by neatly trimming the heel, taking care not to cut into the hard core of the old wood, and then removing any foliage up to one third of its length.

Root Cuttings. These should only be employed as a drastic measure where for various reasons other methods of increase are not suitable; for example, if plants fail to set seed or cannot be struck from ordinary cuttings, or, in some cases where seed is set, the form or variety to be propagated does not breed true. Among this type of plant are the erodiums, *Morisia monantha*, lewisias and *Phlox nana ensifolia* (syn. *P. mesoleuca*).

The strong thick roots of the plant are washed free of soil and cut into pieces $\frac{1}{2}$ to 1 inch in length (smaller sections should be avoided for these will not root). The thickness of the roots to be propagated should not be less than the thickness of a small pencil. The pieces are best inserted in pots, remembering to place the top part upwards (this is important), in a mixture of equal parts of leafmould and sharp sand. They should be positioned so that the top of the cutting is just showing. Another inch of coarse sand is spread over this, the whole pot is well watered and then plunged into a closed frame where fresh growth will soon be discernible. After making steady growth for about a month the young plants should be treated as rooted cuttings and potted on accordingly. These cuttings are best taken in early spring, April and May being ideal months.

Leaf Cuttings. These provide a good method of increase where the plant to be propagated does not form shoots but is of the rosette type. Examples of these are haberleas, ramondas, jankaeas, lewisias, etc. Provided care is taken when removing the leaf there is no reason why one hundred per cent. success should not be achieved. It is necessary to remove any soil or chippings round the base of the plant and the leaf should be held firmly as near to its base as possible, giving it a sharp downward tug so that it comes away complete with its short stalk. This is important for it is in the base of this stalk where it joins the stem that the embryo plant is contained. A pan containing equal parts of well moistened finely sifted leafmould and coarse sand is next prepared and made firm. The leaf cuttings are then laid horizontally on the compost and the short stalk of each is pressed into the mixture and held there either by pinning with a bent piece of wire or, as I consider preferable, a small stone. The pan is then placed in the cutting frame which is kept closed. Rooting invariably takes place quite rapidly but new rosettes are generally slow to form. As soon as there is fresh growth remove the stone and after a further lapse of from four to six weeks the young plants can be potted on in the appropriate compost.

METHODS OF ROOTING CUTTINGS

There are a number of methods in use for the rooting of cuttings but the three main ones which I intend to deal with here are those in general use and by using these the majority of plants can be successfully increased.

The North Frame. The frame which is best suited to the amateur who is only able to attend to it in the evening or early morning, because of business commitments etc., is one that is situated in a cool position, north or north-west for preference, thus needing only occasional attention with regard to watering and so on. By siting the frame in this position the cuttings will take longer to root but this delay is compensated for by the need for watering at only infrequent intervals. During the hot weather it will be necessary to water every day and I think that the best time is in the early morning so that by the time the maximum temperature is reached the atmosphere is nice and humid, an essential condition while the cuttings are forming roots. In cool or rainy weather it will only be necessary to water once a week. A frame of this type situated in a cool, shady spot is essential for the successful rooting of dwarf rhododendrons and other ericaceous plants including, of course, woodlanders.

It is not necessary to use a large frame for rooting cuttings of those plants suitable for cultivating in troughs and sinks, and one for ordinary gardens need only be 3 feet long by 2 feet wide. A frame of this size (which should be placed in a cool position) will hold up to 200 cuttings according to the size of the individual shoots. These frames, constructed of various types of wood, can be bought ready-made and need only siting, but I have a preference for a home-made frame constructed of brick. This type of frame has three advantages over

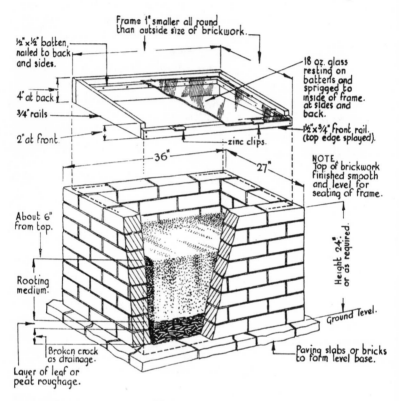

Frame 1" smaller all round than outside size of brickwork.

½"×½" batten, nailed to back and sides.

4" at back

¾" rails

2" at front

18 oz. glass resting on battens and sprigged to inside of frame at sides and back.

1½"×¾" front rail. (top edge splayed).

zinc clips.

NOTE
Top of brickwork finished smooth and level for seating of frame.

36"

27"

Height 24" or as required.

About 6" from top.

Rooting medium.

Ground level.

Broken crock as drainage.

Paving slabs or bricks to form level base.

Layer of leaf or peat roughage.

FIG. 15. *Brick-built propagating frame*

the wooden article; it is almost indestructible, pests are not attracted to it as they are to a wooden frame which is just beginning to decay, and the brick frame has a more constant temperature and humidity content, an essential point where cuttings are trying to form roots. The high humidity means that there is less need for frequent watering and the brick rendering absorbs moisture, giving it off as the temperature of the frame rises during the heat of the day. The body of the frame is constructed of brickwork 4½ inches thick; that is the bricks are laid on the broadest base and built up to 2 feet. The bricks have to be bonded, which means that no join of a course of bricks should be over a join in the course below, and the completed base of the frame should be a sound constructional job. A gap should be left in the bottom tier of the bricks at the lowest end for drainage and a piece of perforated zinc cemented in to prevent the entry of woodlice, slugs, snails, etc. The frame light, which can be bought complete with glass or made at home, should be a close fit as a still, humid atmosphere is essential for rooting cuttings (see Fig. 15).

The cutting frame when completed should be washed down inside with a strong solution of permanganate of potash and, after draining, any surplus cement and rubbish should be removed. It is then filled to a quarter of its depth with rubble or clinker, the larger pieces at the base and the smaller on top until the final layer is quite even. Over the drainage a layer of peat roughage (the residue of sieved horticultural peat) is placed. Often turves are used with the grass face downwards but I do not recommend this method for it is practically impossible to obtain pest-free turves for this purpose. The use of the roughage is to prevent the rooting compost from washing down and blocking the drainage. The remainder of the frame is filled to within 6 inches of the top with a compost made of 2 parts of coarse sand to 1 of moist peat, well mixed together before use. After this compost has been put in the frame it must be well firmed by placing a board on the compost and standing on this. Before use the frame is well watered with a strong solution of permanganate of potash dissolved in boiling water and applied at once. Two teaspoonfuls of crystals to each gallon of water is the strength required. After this a good watering of clean rain water is given, the frame is closed for twenty-four hours to obtain an even temperature, and it is then ready to receive the cuttings.

The Frame in Full Sun. For cultivators who are either retired or able to spend a lot of time in the garden the type of frame I am about to describe has a great advantage over that which I have described above. Cuttings are rooted in a matter of days and a large number of plants can be raised in a short period.

It is a method widely used by commercial growers to whom a quick-rooted cutting is, because of the saving of time, a cheaper selling product. The frame is similar to the brick one just described but it is situated in full sun and the cuttings are inserted in pure sand and kept moist.

A product which the propagator can put to very good use is Vermiculite. This has the amazing property of absorbing up to 200 times its volume in moisture, and thus requires less watering and can be used in place of coarse sand. Care must be taken, however, to obtain the right kind for horticultural work. It is essential that the product should be steeped in water for at least twenty-four hours before being placed in the frame. Adding water to the dry material laid in the frame is useless and a waste of time. A constant watch has to be maintained during the day, never allowing the cuttings to flag or the sand to dry out, so that watering has to be carried out continually throughout the day and every day until rooting has taken place. The cuttings must be removed from the frame as soon as this occurs for both the sand and Vermiculite are sterile, containing no food at all.

Using Bottom Heat. Propagation by bottom heat has always had a good following and in the days before electricity came into general use the hot water pipes in the greenhouse were often utilized for this purpose. The main advantage of this method of rooting cuttings is that it is ideal for the difficult or rare plants, although the easy plants are just as easy, and many plants which cannot be induced to strike by other means are able to form roots with bottom heat. With this method it is, of course, possible to take cuttings at practically any time of the year, and it is especially useful for experimenting with cuttings of plants which are notoriously difficult to root, for by taking cuttings of these plants at different times during both growing and resting periods, it is often possible to induce rooting. To quote an example, *Phlox nana ensifolia* (syn. *P. mesoleuca*) does not set seed or normally strike from cuttings in this country and the only method of propagation has been by root cuttings, hence the rarity of the plant, for not only is the amount of root suitable for propagation small but the parent plant needs great care after this drastic operation. Conducting a series of experiments over a period of six months I found that new shoots placed in a heated frame of this type in late March were rooted by the end of May. I can find no other record of this plant having been rooted from cuttings before.

There are two methods by which electricity can be used to supply bottom heat to a frame. The first is the low voltage soil heater, a resistance wire fed from a step-down transformer from the mains, which is laid on top of the roughage of peat over the drainage in the frame described on p. 53. Naturally, the maker's instructions should be followed but as the current passed is only at a low voltage it is not capable of causing any shock if the cable is handled accidentally. The amount of current consumed depends on the degree of heat required and the size of frame, and the method of regulating the heat is by the length of resistance wire employed. The only drawback I have found in this system is that it can become costly in use over a long period for after the cuttings have been inserted and the current turned on it has to remain on until the cuttings have formed roots.

A more practical and certainly a much more economical frame for the average gardener is one employing an ordinary electric gas-filled lamp which can be of such a wattage as will raise the temperature to the required degree according to the size of frame employed. It is primarily meant to stand on a greenhouse staging but it can also be placed inside an ordinary cold frame where it will function perfectly.

This is a piece of equipment you can make yourself—anybody handy with a saw, drill and screwdriver can build one in a few hours. The construction I will give in detail so that with these notes and the plans (see Fig. 16, overleaf) the handyman can build this heated frame.

Asbestos sheeting, easily obtained from the local builder's yard and just as easy to work, needing only a saw and drill, is ideal for the sides of the frame. This material being non-conductive of heat requires very little current to maintain an equable temperature. A useful size for the frame is 2 feet long by 18 inches wide, the depth at the rear being 18 inches and at the front 15 inches. The supports to hold the asbestos sides are of ½-inch wood, and should be of a hardwood such as oak, teak, etc., or cedar can be used, thus ensuring a long life to the unit which will have to stand up to a very humid atmosphere. Should a softwood, through any circumstances, have to be employed it must be thoroughly treated by soaking in one of the proprietary wood preservatives. A word of warning is needed here to the less experienced cultivators; on no account must creosote or any other preservative with a tar base be used and I have found from personal experience that a copper-based preservative is ideal for this purpose. After treatment cuttings can be inserted without any trace of ill-effect.

The asbestos sheeting after being sawn to shape is drilled and screwed to the wooden supports with ¾-inch screws. The frame light is constructed according to the plan given and should fit tightly when finished. Electric lamps provide the heat supply and in this size of frame a 25-watt lamp will raise the temperature inside by approximately 20°F. above that outside. The holder for this lamp should be of the all-weather type procurable from the local electric supply company and the cable must be strong and durable—that known as cab tyre is ideal for using inside the greenhouse, but if this type of frame is installed in a cold frame outside, suitably earthed, lead-covered

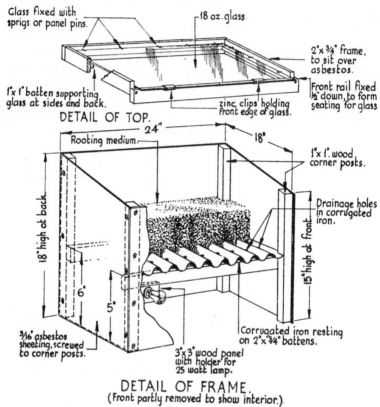

Glass fixed with sprigs or panel pins.

18 oz. glass.

2"x ¾" frame, to sit over asbestos.

1"x 1" batten supporting glass at sides and back.

zinc clips holding front edge of glass.

Front rail fixed ½" down, to form seating for glass.

DETAIL OF TOP.

24"

Rooting medium.

18"

1"x 1" wood corner posts.

18" high at back.

Drainage holes in corrugated iron.

15" high at front.

6"

5"

3/16" asbestos sheeting, screwed to corner posts.

3"x 3" wood panel with holder for 25 watt lamp.

Corrugated iron resting on 2"x ¾" battens.

DETAIL OF FRAME.
(Front partly removed to show interior.)

FIG. 16. *Propagating frame*

cable must be used. The total consumption per week is easily arrived at. Where the cost per unit, that is 1,000 watts, is, say, six pence it means 40 hours heat for that sum, or just over 25 pence per week—a small figure to pay for an easy way of propagating plants which will not root easily by other means.

The frame after siting should be prepared for use by first laying an inch of drainage material, old crocks, broken bricks, etc. and then placing over this a thin covering of roughage (the residue of peat after sieving is suitable); the rooting compost is then added, this consisting of 1 part of sieved garden peat to 2 parts of coarse sand well mixed together. The compost is made firm by pressing with a flat board, not forgetting the corners. The material should be soaked with a solution of permanganate of potash, followed by clean water as advised for the other propagating frame described on p. 53.

When all surplus water has drained away the frame light should be placed in position and the heat turned on; the frame is left for a further twenty-four hours by which time it will have warmed the compost to its maximum heat. A small maximum-minimum thermometer is used to give a reading over any period of time. This is quite easily reset by the use of a magnet supplied with the thermometer. Any great fluctuation must as far as possible be avoided, for a steady temperature is essential for rooting cuttings. The non-conductivity of the asbestos sheeting will do much to minimize any change in outside temperature but if during very cold or prolonged frosty spells the temperature falls below 16°C. (60°F.) a lamp of greater wattage should be installed while the cold spell lasts. An ideal range of temperature in summer is from 16°C. during the night rising to 21°C. (70°F.) by day; in winter the temperature could be 13°C. (55°F.) during the night and 18° C. (65°F.) during the day.

Management of Cutting Frames. As noted in the first part of this chapter the material to be used for cuttings will vary according to the season and type required. For soft green cuttings the top inch or so of the growing shoot can be taken but for both half-hard and fully ripened cuttings it is best pulled away from the parent plant with a quick downward thrust, thus bringing away a little of the old wood which must be trimmed (Fig. 14). If cuttings of half-ripened stock are taken from a position away from the base of the shoot the piece should be cut cleanly (a razor blade fitted in a holder is suitable), just below a node, taking care as with green cuttings that no bruising takes place. The shoot is then prepared by removing all leaves along one third of its length (Fig. 14). There are on the market several kinds of rooting compounds both in powder or liquid form and, used with care, following the maker's instructions, there is no doubt that some have proved of value in rooting difficult cuttings. Where different strengths are required for different types and genera the powder is much easier to use and more economical. Application is very easy and soon becomes routine. All that is required is the dipping of the cutting — the base of which should be dampened beforehand — in the rooting powder to a depth of half an inch. Surplus powder should be gently tapped off and the cutting should be inserted in the frame.

With all types of cuttings care is needed for them to root successfully and like all other gardening jobs attention to detail always pays a dividend. That much abused phrase 'green fingers' is to my mind only another name for care and common sense, for these used together will produce good results. A hole is made with a dibber, large enough to take the cutting so that the base of the cutting rests on the bottom and if the shoot to be propagated is evergreen, when this is resting on the base of the hole the foliage should be just above the surface of the compost. The cutting is then firmed by inserting the blunt end of the dibber in the compost round the cutting and pressing the dibber towards the cutting. The cuttings should be put in rows, close to but not actually touching each other. When all have been dibbed in and firmed they should be well watered in with a watering can fitted with a fine rose to settle the compost round the collars.

When dealing with some of the small cushion plants or those with hairy or felted foliage it is advisable to surface the rooting compost with $\frac{1}{4}$ inch of really sharp silver sand. This is best put on dry just before the cuttings are inserted so that when the holes are made with a dibber a little of the sand trickles to the base of the hole, thus helping to protect both the base and the collar of the cutting from rot. It is at these vital points that rotting invariably takes place.

Labelling is very important for nothing is worse than to take a batch of cuttings, root them successfully, and then a few weeks later find that no names are available. At the time one thinks that one will remember the names of the plants being propagated but I have found to my cost that it is not always so when several species or varieties are involved. There are a number of suitable labels and the old wooden type smeared with white paint, on which the name and date can be written with a garden pencil, has always been a favourite. Another form which is very good is the aluminium strip which can be impressed with a blunt pencil or marked with a waterproof ink. Whichever type is used the name of the plant and the date when the cuttings were taken should be recorded. A label should be placed in front of each batch of cuttings.

Both heated and unheated frames must be kept closed until

rooting has taken place. Water is given every day during spring, summer and early autumn and it is essential to use water that is at the same temperature as that of the frame. Every two weeks a watering of a weak solution of permanganate of potash (about one teaspoonful to two gallons of water) should be given instead of plain water. This will keep in check any growth of liverwort, moss or lichen, which always seems to follow overhead watering. It is beneficial in another way for it is a weak fertilizer and can thus be of use to the cuttings once they are rooted.

A careful watch must be kept for decaying vegetation or cuttings which have begun to rot; these must be removed at once before they set up general decay.

Plants in heated frames should still be watered during the winter months with water which has had the chill taken off it, but those plants in unheated frames should be given only enough water to keep the compost moist and any surplus moisture is best wiped off the frame light. A little air is beneficial during fine winter days. When there are spells of damp, foggy and frosty weather no water should be given.

As soon as the cuttings have rooted they must be potted on into a soil mixture of equal parts loam and leafmould and 2 parts coarse sand. The potted cuttings are then placed in a closed frame until they have become established and new growth is noticed, when air can be given in increasing quantities until the plants are hardened off.

CHAPTER FOUR

PESTS

Equipment, Routine Controls, List of Pests

LIKE all other forms of gardening troughs and sinks have their quota of pests and diseases and precautions must be taken to control an outbreak before it gets out of hand. This is one branch of gardening where prevention is better than cure, for these miniature plants, well able to withstand zero temperatures and other vicissitudes of our uncertain climate, often fall easy prey to an infestation unless a careful watch is maintained. The need for careful attention to this matter is readily understood when it is known that although the plants are small the insects which prey upon them are the same as those which attack plants of normal stature, thus what may be a slight infestation on a specimen 6 feet in height is a major calamity on one of only 6 inches! A regular routine of inspection, spraying and dusting will do much to keep the pests and diseases at bay and possibly arrest what would otherwise be a serious attack—often with disastrous results. There is no doubt that a healthy plant is more resistant to both pests and diseases so that good cultivation will do a great deal towards combating these evils.

Equipment. It will be necessary to obtain a certain amount of equipment for dealing with any outbreak that is likely to occur and the following list should cover the majority of articles required:

Bromophos. A useful granular insecticide for use against a number of soil pests.

Carbaryl. This is now one of the alternatives for the banned D.D.T. It has a useful life of up to two weeks in use and controls woodlice, caterpillars, weevils and leatherjackets.

Dimethoate. A systemic spray which is especially useful against aphids and red spider mite.

H.C.H. An insecticide (formerly known as B.H.C.) which is available in both dust and liquid form and is a good all round control for most pests.

Lime sulphur. This fungicide is obtainable in liquid form for use against mildew.

Nippon'. A sure ant destroyer.

Malathion. A good insecticide available as a spray, dust or aerosol. Do not use on plants belonging to the *Crassulaceae* (*Sedum* and *Sempervivum*).

Pirimophos-methyl. A fairly recent introduction, this is an insecticide which has proved extremely effective in controlling a number of pests. It can be obtained as a dust for the control of woodlice, in liquid form as a spray for red spider mite, scale insects and other pests. It can also be used as a dust or liquid to control springtails, vine weevil grubs and wireworm.

Sulphur. Green and yellow sulphur can be purchased in puffer application packs for use against mildew.

Thiram. A fungicide which will give control of grey mould, mildews and rust.

Spraying machine. For insecticide use a one quart size hand spray with three nozzles.

Routine Controls. A routine should be planned and strictly carried out where practicable which should prevent any serious infestation even at peak periods. It is surprising how easy this is if adhered to.

Before filling the container such as sink, trough, pan, etc., a liberal dusting of HCH powder should be applied over the crocks; this will ensure a clean start. The powder remains effective during its lifetime. Every week from the beginning of April to the end of October (these times are only approximate and can be varied according to both climate and geographical position) a weekly spraying with HCH, alternating with malathion, should be given as directed. These are best applied on dull windy days where possible, but if there is a dry, sunny spell the spraying should be done in the early evening after the sun has passed over the containers. The following morning the plant should be sprayed with clear water to reduce the risk of scorch. If the weather is persistently dry and hot the HCH powder is best applied with a small dusting machine.

During damp, muggy weather and during the later part of the year when there are cold nights after warm days a strict watch should be maintained for mildew and rust and at the first sign of either disease a dusting of sulphur or a lime sulphur spray should be applied.

A liberal dusting of HCH should be given every other week in all cracks and crevices where woodlice, slugs and snails are to be found.

PESTS

A short list of the more common pests likely to be encountered with symptoms and control methods is appended; they may never attack but forewarned is forearmed.

Aphids. The most common is probably the greenfly, but there are many species of aphid. They reproduce rapidly and can quickly transform a healthy plant into a stunted travesty of itself by sucking out the sap.

Symptoms. Plants look unhealthy, all parts are stunted and mal-formed and the pests can be plainly seen, a congested mass on all parts of the specimen.

Control. Spray with either HCH or malathion, followed by a clear water spray the following day. Repeat the dose every other day until the plants are free.

Woodlice, Earwigs, Slugs and **Snails.** These are nocturnal feeders and should be looked for after dark—or in cracks and crevices during the daytime.

Symptoms. Growth of the plant above the soil surface is badly eaten, or on removing a plant which has suddenly collapsed it is found that the roots have been eaten away. The latter damage is due to woodlice.

Control. Hand picking after dark is advised for slugs and snails, but a liberal dusting of HCH powder in all cracks and crevices will do much to keep all these pests at bay.

Red Spider. This can be a real pest in dry seasons for it thrives and multiplies rapidly under these conditions.

Symptoms. A lens is needed to see these mites for they are extremely small, but if the foliage of the plant has a mottled appearance, etched with fine white lines, then it is almost certain that it is being attacked by this pest.

Control. Regular spraying with malathion or dimethoate, making sure that all parts of the plant are moistened, especially the undersides of the leaves. These sprays should be followed by one of clear water, keeping the affected plant moist during treatment, a condition which s not favourable to the red spider mite.

Thrips. A very small insect, not easily seen. Extremely active, especially when disturbed.

Symptoms. Distorted foliage, deformed buds and flowers.

Control. Powdered naphthalene should be sprinkled on the surface of the soil, at the rate of about 2 oz. to the square yard; this, with the routine spray, should keep this pest at bay.

Springtails. Most likely to be found where the conditions are moist and damp, such as in seed pans or when the 'billiard table' form of gardening is adopted. They are small, greyish-black, wingless insects with pronounced antennae, and they jump when disturbed.

Symptoms. Leaves eaten from small plants, seedlings collapse due to the stem being eaten at soil level.

Control. As for thrips.

Scale Insects. The hardwood plants are sometimes affected by these pests which can be a serious menace unless checked.

Symptoms. Black marking on the foliage. A plant showing this symptom should be examined with a lens for any brownish-grey, shell-like humps on the stems, for these are the protective coverings for these insects.

Control. A spray of petroleum oil, then a proprietary insecticide should be used as directed.

Caterpillars. Very destructive pests which can do untold damage in a short time.

Symptoms. Leaves partially eaten away and gummed together to form a cocoon.

Control. The routine spraying of HCH or malathion, or hand picking where noticed will do much to keep these pests in check.

Ants. These can do a lot of harm in a small trough or sink with their tunnelling habits, thus disturbing the roots of the plants.

Symptoms. The plants look unhealthy, and a mound of fine soil is thrown up round the plants.

Control. A little 'Nippon' is placed in the run of the ants and they take this to their nests for food, thus quickly spreading this poison and destroying a complete nest almost overnight.

Earthworms. These also cause damage by earth disturbance, mor noticeable in a container.

Symptoms. Their presence is noted by the small humps of blac earth on the surface of the soil.

Control. The only really effective measure is to water the containe with a strong solution of permanganate of potash; this will bring th worms to the surface.

Birds. These can be extremely destructive, especially to the cushio plants and early spring-flowering bulbs.

There is no effective method of getting rid of them and the only remedy is either to cage the trough with wire netting or thread black cotton on sticks across the containers.

Armeria caespitosa Bevan's Variety, a compact form of deeper colouring than the species (see p. 90).

Calceolaria Walter Shrimpton, a superb hybrid bred from *C. darwinii* and *C. fothergillii* (see p. 129). This hybrid is much easier to grow than its parents.

Campanula raineri, a choice campanula from the Central European Alps (see p. 91).

Dianthus arvernensis, a delightful, late-flowering species which is native to central France (see p. 130).

THE PLANTS

CHAPTER FIVE

INTRODUCTION

IN compiling this list of suitable plants I have borne in mind the needs both of beginners and of the more advanced cultivators, for after all the expert of today was the novice of yesterday so that it is desirable and necessary to include both easy and difficult plants.

Naturally, the more advanced gardener tends to specialize and here is an ideal medium in which to experiment, for with trough cultivation it is possible to devote separate troughs to each genus, growing a combination of species and varieties. Thus, in due season, individual troughs will present an outstanding display of floral beauty.

It is not possible or desirable to give instructions as to what are the best plants to be grown together; this form of gardening calls for individual likes and dislikes and each trough, like a landscape in paint, must be the creation of the cultivator. All that I can do is to generalize and, by a careful study of the following tables, combinations of colour, height, spread and form with approximate time of flowering will give the necessary aid in producing the landscapes in miniature.

The time of flowering given can only be approximate for conditions vary from district to district; the western seaboard may be a week or so ahead of the southern counties, which in turn can be up to a month ahead of the North-East and Scottish Highlands.

If it is desired to have small troughs filled with flowering plants for indoor decoration at one time such as early spring, this can be arranged quite easily by choosing the species and varieties which normally flower together. For example, complete units can be built up containing a collection of the dwarf Kabschia or Engleria saxifrages, or, say, early-flowering crocus species and varieties of miniature narcissi, and ideal decorations for the dreary winter months are pans or small oblong sinks filled with the many different kinds of dwarf sempervivums which seem to thrive on neglect, even showing greater foliage coloration under these conditions.

The illustrations of the troughs in this book will repay study for all are well-established units of growing plants from several gardens of leading amateurs in this country who have devoted much care and thought to their construction, and for beginners who are feeling

67

their way in this method of cultivating alpine plants, planting on similar lines to start with will provide a good basis from which individual tastes will develop as experience is gained.

Position is of some importance for it is bound up with soil, rainfall and other local conditions, including the district in which the troughs are situated, and to interpret the tables intelligently allowance must be made for these widely differing conditions. These tables are compiled primarily for the southern counties where conditions are normally drier than in other parts of the country, so that where shade is indicated for the South, half shade in the Midlands and even full sun in the North, where the atmosphere contains a great deal of moisture, would possibly be more suitable.

Nomenclature. Unfortunately it is not possible to give these plants common names which could be easily remembered and would also mean the same to gardeners in different localities. After all, the bluebell of Scotland is a campanula, whereas in England it is a wild hyacinth. This is but one example but it could be repeated over and over again. Anyone who is willing to take the trouble to cultivate these plants should also be prepared to learn their botanical names; it is surprising how soon the average gardener not only learns but also remembers the names and this leads to acceptance among the brotherhood of gardeners, often opening up correspondence with gardeners of the wide world to whom an androsace or a saxifrage is always the same whether the cultivator speaks French, Russian, German or any other language.

The Royal Horticultural Society's *Dictionary of Gardening*, to which acknowledgment is made, has been used as the basis for naming the plants listed in these pages. Other botanical references have been consulted in respect of the plants now added to the book in Appendix 1 (see p.128). A number of plants listed here will not be found in the *Dictionary*; this is because I have endeavoured to include all plants known today, and among these are a number of new and rare plants often only found in specialist collections and a number now being propagated by leading nurserymen which should become available shortly.

Where, as often happens, old-established names have been changed because of the belated discovery of earlier published names and descriptions, which under the International Rules of Nomenclature have priority, cross references have been made or the old names retained as synonyms. Those readers concerned that they should be completely up to date regarding nomenclature should turn to Appendix 2 (p.133) where the latest name changes are recorded.

It will often be found that nurserymen — who, after all, sell plants for a living—are loth to change plant names which are well known for names which mean nothing to a large number of gardeners, so if it is found when ordering plants that a particular plant is not listed under the name given priority in this work, remember that it may be listed under the old name or synonym.

The conifers have been dealt with more fully for there is no other group of miniature plants among which there is so much confusion in nomenclature. Much has been done by reputable nurserymen to weed out the undesirables but where the public demands a mature plant for quite a small sum there will always be a supply of unsuitable material available. Too often the dwarf of today is the giant of tomorrow so always demand a conifer on its own roots, but also be prepared to pay a reasonable price for what is possibly up to three years' labour or more on the part of the nurseryman.

CHAPTER SIX

DWARF CONIFERS

Position, Cultivation, Suitable Species and Forms

Of all the plants for trough and sink cultivation none is more suitable than the dwarf conifers; possibly this is due to both being to a certain extent artificial means to an end. These miniatures —which, with few exceptions, are not true species but abnormal seedlings or sports from natural-growing forest trees in the form of witches' brooms—are used extensively in the rock garden, but always need care in placing. They will, however, improve enormously the appearance of the sink or trough in which they are planted. If ever a plant was made to measure for this form of gardening the dwarf conifer was, and, provided care is taken in selection and placing, nothing is more satisfying and pleasing to the eye. They are obtainable in all sizes and shapes—rounded, compact balls of dense congested branches; open branchlets covered with feathery foliage; gnarled, contorted trunks, age-old in appearance; upright columnar-shaped trees tapering to the apex; and pendent and prostrate forms moulding themselves to the rocks over which they grow. Colours vary from cream through yellow-green and every shade of green to deep green, browns in almost every hue, often from light to deep, and there are even silvery-white forms. In fact, all are interesting throughout the whole year.

There are, of course, pitfalls and this is the main reason for devoting a complete chapter to these miniatures. First of all I should like to issue a warning: all dwarf conifers must, and I repeat must, be on their own roots. Grafted plants are to be avoided at all costs for they will, within a few years, lose all their natural dwarf characteristics and become unbalanced, unsightly plants which remain eyesores until removed. Secondly, these plants are not cheap, for it takes many years to bring to maturity a specimen of any size. Such is the extremely slow growth of these plants that the bun forms of *Chamaecyparis obtusa* will take twenty years to make a plant only 3 inches high by 6 to 8 inches across. So do not blame the nurseryman who, to get plants of reasonable size to sell at an economic price, has to graft or be accused of sending out a rooted cutting which in reality can be up to three years old. Conifers advertised as dwarfs 6 to 9 inches high for, say, 50p each, must be looked upon with suspicion for a true dwarf this size could be 30 years old and the price would be reckoned in pounds, not pence! Do not let this put you off these delightful dwarfs, for nothing is more interesting and satisfying than to watch a miniature conifer grow to maturity from a small cutting.

No satisfactory explanation has yet been given as to why a normal tree anything up to 100 to 150 feet in height can produce seedlings which are only a few feet high when grown to their full size in a period of from 20 to 50 years, and what is just as strange is the fact that seedlings produced from these dwarfs will very rarely breed dwarf offspring but will revert to natural forest trees. Like everything else there are exceptions to the rule and occasionally outstanding new varieties appear. For example the bun forms of *Chamaecyparis obtusa* were raised from seed set from *C.o. nana gracilis*, itself far from dwarf.

The only other method by which dwarf forms are obtained is from what are commonly known as witches' brooms—these are abnormal growths appearing generally at the end of a branch in the form of a congested mass of twigs, as unlike the parent plant as anything could possibly be. Their cause is to a large extent unknown but two theories have been put forward; one is that they are due to narrowing of the sap cells causing abnormal growth and the other that insects injuring the bark cause constriction of the sap. Whatever the cause, cuttings taken from these abnormal shoots will breed true and retain their dwarf habit.

Nomenclature of these plants is very confused and care will have to be taken that a collection of names is not bought; when I state that it is possible to grow three entirely different plants from one specimen it will be readily seen why there are so many synonyms. From a plant of *Chamaecyparis lawsoniana ellwoodii,* itself a charming plant, I took cuttings from the base, from halfway up the plant and from the apex. The plants from the basal cuttings retained their dwarf habit and grew very slowly; those from half-way up were much taller, while the apex plants were unrecognizable when compared with the parent plant. Propagation too from the different types of foliage, juvenile, intermediate and adult, from the same plant will also produce three entirely different plants. This can go on almost *ad infinitum,* plunging the naming of these plants into chaos which it would need a lifetime's work to straighten out.

Until experience is gained in knowing what to obtain, a reliable nurseryman specializing in these dwarf conifers should be consulted, or visits should be made to shows of the Alpine Garden Society, which numbers among its members some of the greatest experts on dwarf conifers in this country. At these shows there are always classes for these dwarf specimens. The conifers on show are as correctly named as possible under present circumstances, and a study of the specimens will soon give the collector ideas of what to look for when purchasing plants. There is one infallible test when looking for dwarf conifers for troughs and sinks: that is to visit a nursery specializing in these miniatures in the first week or so in June for by this time new growth is generally completed. This growth is quite distinct from the previous year's growth and the amount on the specimen will immediately give the yearly increase of the size of the plant. A little mental arithmetic will enable the prospective purchaser to judge the suitability of the specimen under review for any given size of trough or sink and its ultimate size can be computed for a period of years.

Choosing Sites. Position is important with some of the dwarf types; all the 'buns' require a little shade during the hottest part of the day in the South of England and where the atmosphere is dry, but this is not so important in the North and Scotland where it is much more humid. A number of these conifers are surface rooters and require this protection or they will soon show their dislike of these conditions by turning brown. The use of rocks suitably placed over the roots on the surface of the compost, preferably so that they afford protection when the sun is highest, will do much to minimize any danger to the plants. The junipers, pines and cedars are avid sun-lovers and can be planted in full sun with confidence. One of the finest combinations I have ever seen was a shallow trough completely planted with the cobweb houseleek, *Sempervivum arachnoideum,* and three fastigiate junipers, *Juniperus communis compressa,* a sight which has to be seen to be believed. Draughty positions should be avoided as far as possible and protection from cold east winds is advisable; a little forethought when siting the troughs will ensure this.

A collection of these conifers planted in a trough or sink (which should be large enough to take at least a dozen specimens) will provide a picture that will harmonize with any type of surroundings during spring and summer when there is plenty of floral colour, although with the different hues of the conifers themselves the trough will present a charming landscape in miniature. It is when the dreary lays of winter are upon us that a trough so planted will be a never-nding source of delight.

Cultivation. All the dwarf conifers listed here can be grown quite easily in any of the standard composts advocated for the different kinds of sinks and troughs. Lime is not essential and the plants will grow well in a neutral or limy medium. If the contents of the trough—especially plants such as *Phyteuma comosum* and *Campanula zoysii*—demand lime for their well-being, and it is proposed to plant a dwarf conifer in the trough containing plants of this type to break what would otherwise be a flat, unbroken surface, a little leafmould mixed in the compost where the conifer is to be planted will neutralize any excessive lime. A periodic top-dressing of equal parts of leafmould, loam and coarse sand should be spread and watered in round the surface of the chippings near where the conifer is planted. This top-dressing is best given in early September and again in spring; early April is a suitable time. Where the composts are normal or even where they consist predominantly of humus, such as for the 'billiard table' in which dwarf ericaceous plants are grown, and a conifer or two is placed to give suitable shade to some choice plant during the hottest hours of the day, no extra leafmould will be needed. Top-dressing is carried out for all troughs in which conifers are planted, as noted above.

Pruning. There should not in general be any need for pruning these dwarf growing conifers but sometimes the dwarf forms will tend to throw an abnormal shoot or leader which by its appearance suggests that it will dominate the plant if it is allowed to remain. A judicious pinching back of excess growth can be done to keep a nicely balanced specimen. The use of the knife or secateurs should be avoided as much as possible for the natural growth invariably is more beautiful than man's handiwork.

Propagation. With the exception of the genera *Cedrus* and *Pinus*, which can be increased by layering, all dwarf conifers can be increased by cuttings, thus eliminating the need for grafting with its attendant perils of producing quick-growing specimens. To digress for a moment, I know a number of my gardening friends are going to raise their eyebrows after reading the last sentence, but I say to them: plant those grafted specimens that grow so well in pots, with their consequent root restriction, outside in a trough or large container and watch the result. If in a year or so they have not begun to lose their dwarf characteristics then I will eat my hat! For all dwarf forms whether they are from shoots, witches' brooms or abnormal seedlings, vegetative reproduction is the only means of increasing the stock. Even if the plants set fertile seed the resultant plants will, unless the million to one chance produces a new dwarf form, be like their forebears—forest trees.

All cuttings should be taken from the base of the plant for, as explained earlier in this chapter, cuttings from any other parts of the plant will very likely result in a specimen which will not only be larger than its parent but also different. By all means take cuttings from different parts of the plant if there is any purpose in so doing but also keep a record, for too much haphazard propagation has been done which is one of the reasons why the nomenclature of these dwarf conifers is so confusing, with its welter of synonyms.

The cuttings are pulled away from the parent plant with a slight downward tug so that a sliver of the old wood is also attached. This should be trimmed back, taking care that the core where the cutting left the branch is not cut into.

For rooting in a north-facing frame as described in Chapter Three (see p. 51) the cuttings are best taken in late August; these will have callused by the beginning of May and should be well rooted by the end of September the following year. They should be left in the propagating frame and potted up the next spring in equal parts of loam, leafmould and sand. If quick rooting is required, and for the more difficult forms the heated frame is the answer, both green cuttings taken in June or well-ripened cuttings in August will root in a short period.

Layering is the only way of propagating vegetatively members of the genera *Cedrus* and *Pinus* for they are extremely difficult, if not impossible, to root by cuttings. I shall, therefore, give details of this method. It is a slow but normally successful way, carried out in early spring, and the conifer to be used for propagation purposes must first of all have any chippings removed from around its base and replaced with a compost of equal parts of loam, leafmould and coarse sand. The branch to be used for layering is then bent down and where the shoot touches the soil it is stripped of all foliage from that point back to where it joins the parent plant. A slight upward cut is then made in the shoot at soil level and it is pegged down with a strong metal peg so that it cannot move. The shoot is then covered with

he compost up to approximately an inch above and below the cut
and a large stone is placed on top, to keep the shoot in position and
to help to keep the surrounding soil moist. At no time must the soil
be allowed to dry out while rooting is taking place, a procedure which
may take up to two years. A further two months must elapse and
then the cutting can be severed from the parent plant; after a further
period the shoot may be lifted and potted up in equal parts of leafmould, loam and sand and placed in a closed cold frame until it has
become established.

SUITABLE SPECIES AND FORMS

As a foreword to a list of dwarf conifers suitable for cultivation in
troughs and sinks I would like to say that all those noted here can be
planted in the confidence that they will not outgrow their allotted
space in the prostrate forms or become too high in the upright specimens for at least fifteen years, provided that they are growing on
their own roots and are not grafted. If, when planting a trough, small
specimens are used and it is necessary for these to remain dwarfer
than they would normally, do not take them out of their pots but
sink the pots in the compost and cover their rims with chippings to
hide them. The pots will cause a certain amount of root restriction
and so affect the rate of growth, and, provided care is taken when
watering to see that the water is placed round the base of the tree,
thus ensuring that the roots confined inside the small pot are moist,
the plant will come to no harm.

Gardeners must not be disappointed if all the plants listed here are
not easily obtainable; many are rare due to several causes, among
them the difficulty of propagation and the extreme slowness of growth.
Most of them can be found even if it means a little searching in out-
of-the-way nurseries. All the dwarf conifers mentioned here are in
cultivation in this country at the time of writing.

Abies

Of the abies only two are in general cultivation in this country,
and both are forms of the balsam fir, a native of North-East America.

A. balsamea hudsonia.

An extremely rare dwarf form which originated at high altitudes in the White Mountains, New Hampshire, America. A descrip-

tion is given of this and the following form to avoid confusion between the two.

Branches growing at an angle of 60°. Leaves deep bright green above, beneath marked with two depressed blue lines with leaf edges and midrib of deep dark green. Annual growth between ½ and ¾ inch.

A. balsamea nana (syn. *A.b. globosa nana*).

An even rarer plant than the previous form; in fact, *A.b. hudsonia* is often sold under this name. Branches at not more than an angle of 40°. The leaves are bent in a slight arc from base to apex, not straight; bright green above, pale yellow beneath, edged with two white depressed bands separated by a raised yellow-green midrib. Annual growth up to ½ inch. The synonym *globosa nana* derives its name from a form which is identical with the type, the only difference being that it tends to be more rounded in shape.

Cedrus

The cedars have produced three dwarf forms but only two are suitable for trough culture, both being forms of *C. libani* (syn. *C. libanitica*, *C. libanotica*) the Cedar of Lebanon. The third, a native of Cyprus, *C. brevifolia* (syn. *C. libani brevifolia*) can be used if due allowance is made that it will reach approximately 2 feet 6 inches in ten years, but growth can be restricted if it is planted in its pot as a young plant.

C. libani Comte de Dijon.

An extremely rare plant. *C. brevifolia* is often sent out from nurseries under this name. It is easily distinguished from that form in being of a close pyramidical habit with slightly ascending branches densely clothed with fine, needle-shaped leaves about ½ inch in length tapering to base and apex, deep green and slightly hairy. *C. brevifolia* has horizontal branches, less crowded leaves, smaller, not tapered, slightly incurved and almost rounded. Growth is less than 1 inch a year.

C. libani nana.

This is another dwarf form, less compact than the previous one but more rounded. Leaves deep dark green up to 1 inch in length, not hairy but very coarse. Annual growth about 1 inch.

Chamaecyparis

For a great number of years this genus has been known and distributed under the name *Cupressus*, and even today there are many urserymen who are still sending out these plants labelled *Cupressus*. The chief difference between the two genera, *Chamaecyparis,* the false cypress, and *Cupressus,* the true cypress, is that *Chamaecyparis* has flattened and more saucer-shaped branches with small cones while in *Cupressus* the branches are more rounded with larger cones. What were once called retinosporas are now included in *Chamaecyparis,* for these are nothing more than varieties of the latter which have retained their juvenile foliage. There is no doubt that this genus has provided the largest number of plants which are suitable for troughs or sinks for they are certainly, in the *obtusa* forms, the slowest growing of all conifers. The bun-shaped varieties of *C. obtusa nana gracilis* were raised in the nurseries of W. H. Rogers, Southampton, from seedlings of this dwarf conifer and there are no forms in cultivation today which can surpass these miniatures.

C. lawsoniana fletcheri nana.

The form *fletcheri* is a tall-growing conifer of columnar habit reaching 6 feet in about 10 years but often listed by nurserymen as a true dwarf, so beware! However, this dwarf form of it is a charming plant, rounded in habit, with juvenile foliage, beautiful glaucous green intensely crowded and feathery. The origin of this form is unknown but I suspect that it is a cutting taken from the base of a plant of *fletcheri* growing on its own roots, with juvenile foliage. Annual growth less than 1 inch a year.

The species *C. obtusa* is a native of Japan and like so many other famous plants was introduced to Europe by the Victorian nurseryman J. G. Veitch, in 1861. There are a number of dwarf forms and seedlings which have been established in cultivation, and the following are ideal for troughs and sinks.

C. obtusa caespitosa.

A 'bun' form of *obtusa*, making a rounded globe of very compact branches well dotted with the blunted, adpressed, bright green leaves. Annual growth ½ inch.

C.o. compacta.

One of the more suitable specimens for trough culture, being extremely slow growing; from my experience, a plant over 20 years old would not be more than 8 inches across by 3 inches in height, so that the annual growth is negligible. It is a tightly congested mass of saucer-shaped branchlets of deep green foliage.

C.o. ericoides (syn. *C.o. sanderi*).

This dwarf form retains its juvenile foliage. Branches thick, leaves small, congested in threes, blunt at apex, incurved, flat on top, convex underneath; the whole forming a rounded bush rather flat on top. An attractive plant on account of the coloration of its leaves, these being of a shiny blue-green in spring and summer, turning to a delightful purple-red in winter. This plant needs careful placing away from cold winds, and should be given protection from the early morning sun after late spring frosts. Annual growth approximately ½ inch.

C.o. juniperoides.

Another dwarf form but not quite so close in formation as *ericoides*, though it is near to the form *pygmaea,* with scale-like narrow leaves, rounded and less adpressed than in the form *caespitosa.*

C.o. minima (syn. *C. tetragona minima*).

Possibly the smallest of all dwarf conifers, with its bun-shaped congested mass of bright green leaves on smaller upright branches. Annual growth is almost imperceptible.

C.o. nana.

Nothing is more delightful than this dwarf form of the species, if obtained true to name. Unfortunately, *C.o.n. gracilis* is often sent out for this plant and this is a much more vigorous plant, not suitable for troughs. It is easily distinguished for the leaves of the variety *nana* are of a dark, dull green while those of *gracilis* are a bright, deep green. Branches fan-shaped, not so congested as in the other forms, but more open. Annual growth less than 1 inch.

C.o.n. kosteri.

A form which originated in Holland from the nurseries of M. Koster and Sons, Boskoop, Holland, which differs from *nana* in being smaller, more compact. The congested, adpressed leaves are brownish-green. Annual growth less than 1 inch.

C.o. pygmaea.

This plant must not be confused with the variety *pygmaea* of the

ade which is prostrate, spreading, open-fan shaped, making a large
lant in width at least, in a short time. The true plant is intermediate
etween the varieties *nana* and *n. kosteri,* with foliage similar to
icoides, brownish in colour, congested, scale-like, but not adpressed.
nnual growth less than 1 inch. Before buying I would advise any-
ody who is uncertain about this plant to go, if possible, to the Royal
Horticultural Society's Wisley Garden, near Woking in Surrey where
ne alpine house contains an outstanding specimen of the true plant.

C. pisifera (syn. *Cupressus pisifera, Retinospora pisifera*).

The type species introduced by J. G. Veitch from Japan is much
oo large for trough culture but it has produced four suitable forms.

C.p. nana.

An extremely slow-growing conifer and the smallest of all the *pisi-
era* forms; growth less than ½ inch yearly. Prostrate, flat-topped, con-
ested bushlet with fan-shaped branches thickly covered with the
lark bluish-green leaves.

C.p. nana aurea variegata.

Similar to the above but more rounded and densely crowded with
he variegated golden-green foliage. A very desirable plant.

C.p. plumosa compressa (syn. *C.p. plumosa nana compressa*).

A very small form of *plumosa,* making a cushion of both juvenile
nd intermediate minute foliage of a bright glaucous green. Growth
ess than 1 inch yearly.

C.p. squarrosa minima.

This is a plant which, although in cultivation, is not easy to obtain;
ut it is worth searching for. It is slow growing, spreading outwards
ather than upwards; foliage in whorls of three, feathery, tapering to
point, glaucous green, underneath two white lines. Annual growth
ess than 1 inch.

Cryptomeria

The Japanese Cedar, *C. japonica,* which was introduced into Europe
bout 1844, has produced two forms which are suitable for cultivation
n troughs and sinks. Strangely enough both varieties originated in
Japan for there seems to be no trace of any dwarf forms appearing in

Europe. Both these plants need careful placing for they are ver
susceptible to cold and drying winds.

C. japonica Bandai-Sugi.

A good dwarf conifer of close, compact habit growing more i
width than height, with both long and short branchlets dense
crowded with the rather thick needles. Of a bright bluish-gree
turning to a fine reddish-brown in winter due to the coloration of th
tips of the leaves. Annual growth less than 1 inch.

C.j. vilmoriniana.

An astonishing plant which was brought to this country by Murra
Hornibrook in 1923 from Les Verriers, France, where it had bee
introduced from Japan by M. Philippe de Vilmorin about 35 year
before and after whom it was named.

It is absolutely necessary to have this variety on its own roots for i
to retain its dwarf habit. Grafted plants will within a year or s
begin to throw abnormal leaders from different parts of the plan
Care is needed when buying for far too often *C. japonica compacta*,
much more vigorous and taller growing plant, is sent out. The tru
plant is extremely slow growing, not more than $\frac{3}{4}$ inch a year, wit
short, very stout branchlets densely crowded with the minute sti
leaves, dark green in colour.

Dacrydium

D. laxifolium.

This is a true species from New Zealand and endemic to that coun
try, where it is found in both the North and South Islands. It form
a delightful prostrate shrublet with wiry horizontal spreading
branches, its annual growth being less than 1 inch. Leaves in th
juvenile state are open, pointed, curved, quite lax, tapering to th
apex. When mature the leaves are more crowded, very thick, no
pointed and overlapping on the stems, the whole a deep glossy green
Requires a sunny position and shelter from cold winds.

Juniperus

A fairly large race of conifers, the junipers have produced two dwar
forms both suitable for our purpose. The Noah's Ark juniper, *J
communis compressa*, is known under many varietal names, but all are
near enough to be classified under *compressa* while the rare and very

An outstanding specimen of *Draba rigida*, a species from Armenia (see p. 95).

Dryas octopetala minor, the small form of a fine Scottish native (see p. 95).

Edraianthus pumilio, a cushion-forming member of the campanula family from Dalmatia (see p. 95).

Genista delphinensis, one of the best of the miniature brooms and a native of southern France (see p. 98).

lesirable hedgehog juniper, *J. communis echiniformis*, is truly named,
bearing more than a passing resemblance to that animal both in
appearance and touch.

. communis compressa (syn. *J.c. hibernica compressa, J. compressa*).

This is the one conifer which is always noted in all articles on
rough gardens, no doubt on account of its columnar habit which
gives the final touch to a landscape in miniature. It forms an upright,
perfectly symmetrical column of closely congested upright branches
densely clothed with the needle-shaped leaves in whorls of three,
bright glaucous green in colour. Annual growth can be as little as a
$\frac{1}{4}$ inch in poor soil and never more than 1 inch in a better medium.
This is a plant which appreciates a sunny position and looks well when
situated among a collection of sempervivums.

J.c. echiniformis (syn. *J. echiniformis*).

The hedgehog juniper is rare in cultivation but worth searching
for as it is certainly one of the best dwarf conifers and is also extremely
slow growing, making less than $\frac{1}{2}$ inch of new growth yearly. It
makes a small rounded bush of ascending branches densely packed
with needle-shaped foliage, pointed and sharp to the touch, of a
deep bright green. Needs protection from cold winds.

Microcachrys

M. tetragona.

This is a monotypic species from Tasmania where it inhabits the
summits of the Western Range and Mount Lapeyrouse. It is a quite
prostrate dwarf conifer spreading horizontally, never above 1 inch
or so in height, stems brownish-red, closely packed with mid-green
adpressed leaves. It is often mistaken for one of the New Zealand
whipcord veronicas or, to be botanically correct, hebes, and the
annual growth is less than 1 inch. The flowers of both sexes are borne
at the apex of individual shoots and the resultant delightful miniature
cones are only $\frac{1}{4}$ inch in length, dark orange in colour.

Picea

Of the many dwarf varieties which the Norway spruce has produced
there are very few which are really suitable for cultivation in troughs,
for most will grow too large over a period of years. Care has to be
taken in buying these forms for there is a great deal of confusion in

their naming. A large majority are practically indistinguishable from each other.

P. abies echiniformis (syn. *Abies excelsa echiniformis*).

This is a dwarf variety but it is not quite so slow growing as *P.a. humilis* (see below). The annual rate of increase is up to 1 inch. It makes a low mound of ascending, pale brown branches and congested, needle-shaped foliage of a light yellow-green.

P.a. gregoryana (syn. *Abies excelsa gregoryana*).

This makes a close, congested mound of small individual humps, branches small and spreading, white in colour. Leaves small, narrow, needle shaped, arranged round the pale grey-green branches. Annual growth not more than $\frac{1}{2}$ inch.

Of all the dwarf conifers this is a plant which is seldom found true, many other forms of *P. abies* doing duty for it. There is one infallible test for the type plant and that is that the leaves are always found radially arranged *all*, and the emphasis is on the word *all*, over the plant.

P.a. humilis (syn. *Abies excelsa humilis, P. excelsa humilis*).

This variety has an annual rate of growth of only about $\frac{1}{4}$ inch. It makes a small, roundish compact bushlet of congested, small, ascending branches densely covered with the very small, dark shiny green, thickish leaves.

P.a. pygmaea (syn. *Abies excelsa pygmaea, P. excelsa gregoryana*).

A charming and extremely slow-growing conifer of rounded habit with ascending, silver-white branches crowded with the small, stout leaves of yellow-green. Growth less than 1 inch yearly.

P. albertiana conica.

A charming dwarf of narrow pyramidal growth with fine springy branches of a bright light yellow. Leaves thin and long, arranged unevenly round the branches terminating in a point, light glaucous green. This plant needs protection from cold winds. Annual rate of growth under 1 inch.

Pinus

Although there are a large number of pines only a few are really suitable for trough culture, but if the following larger growing species are planted as small specimens in pots into the trough they will remain quite dwarf for a number of years. Care must be taken that they are not planted in troughs whose other occupants will resent root disturbance when the time comes for the conifers to be removed. The species that can be utilized for this purpose are *P. albicaulis, P. cembra, P. cembroides monophylla* and *P. parviflora*.

P. cembra pygmaea.

An extremely slow-growing conifer from a dwarf seedling of the Arolla Pine. Its close, contorted branches are densely covered with grey-green, curved, slender leaves borne in fives. Annual rate of growth about $\frac{1}{4}$ inch.

P. parviflora brevifolia.

The species is used by the Japanese to produce the delightful artificially dwarfed trees, an art at which they are past masters. This form which originated in Japan and was introduced to Europe in 1890, is in itself a dwarf-growing conifer needing no artificial methods of growth restriction for it to retain its dwarf habit.

It forms a small, prostrate, slightly rounded, compact bush of crowded branches bearing the densely packed bundles of five curved leaves, bright green above, white beneath. Growth about $\frac{1}{2}$ inch yearly.

Pinus pumila (syn. *P. pygmaea*).

This, the smallest pine in cultivation today, is often listed as the Japanese form of *P. cembra* but it is a true species and endemic to Japan although there are reports of it being found in Siberia. It is similar to the foregoing which often does duty for it. The only difference between the two plants is a minute botanical one; in *P. cembra pumila* the marginal serrulations are constant whereas in *P. pumila* the leaves are often entire and lacking in marginal serrulations. Annual growth almost imperceptible.

P. sylvestris beauvronensis.

The Scots Pine, a native of these Isles, has produced a few dwarf forms but only one is suitable for trough culture. *P. sylvestris beauvronensis* is believed to have originated as a 'witches' broom' but there is no definite record to bear out this statement.

It makes a very compact, densely crowded mass of right-angled branches clothed with shiny green leaves borne in twos along the branchlets. Annual rate of growth approximately 1 inch.

Taxus

The yews have a reputation for longevity and slow growing yet they have produced very few dwarf forms and there is only one which can be considered as suitable for our purpose.

T. baccata pygmaea.

A very slow-growing form which came from the famous conifer nurseries of Messrs Den Ouden, Boskoop, Holland. It forms a shallow, almost oval bush of closely compressed upright branches, crowded with the oval, grey-green leaves which are stiff and recurved. Annual rate of growth less than ½ inch.

Thuja

The dwarf forms of *T. orientalis*, the Chinese Arbor-vitae, introduced into Europe in the late eighteenth century, are ideal plants for the rock garden but there are, unfortunately, only two which can be used for trough culture. Both are fine plants and only need care in placing (for they are intolerant of drying winds and drought) to give colour and grace to any trough.

T. orientalis meldensis (syn. *Biota meldensis*).

A rare dwarf conifer of close, compact habit forming a more or less rounded shrub of semi-erect branches, spreading and densely clothed with opposite, needle-shaped, glaucous green leaves. The whole plant turns to reddish-purple in winter. Annual rate of growth less than 1 inch.

T. orientalis minima glauca (syn. *Biota orientalis minima glauca*).

Another small conifer which is slower growing than the foregoing variety, making a very dense congested rounded 'bun' of ascending branches, densely covered with the fine, needle-shaped foliage of grey-green, turning to yellow-brown in winter. Growth is not more than ½ inch yearly.

CHAPTER SEVEN

DESCRIPTIVE LIST OF PLANTS

A FEW abbreviations have been used in compiling the Descriptive List of Plants in order to make it possible to provide all the required information at a glance in a condensed form, without the unnecessary repetition of words which would make this work too large and unwieldy.

I will explain these abbreviations in the order in which they appear in the columns of the Descriptive List:

Name. First is the name of the genus to which the plant belongs, given in capitals. Under the generic name the names of the species and varieties are recorded. If the word synonym, abbreviated to syn., is placed before the specific or varietial name it means the plant in question may be found under that name in nurserymen's catalogues.

If the genus has been changed then it will be noted; for example

ANEMONE
halleri   See *Pulsatilla halleri*

Suitability. Under this heading a general idea is given of the best container to grow the plant in.

A. This signifies that the plant can be grown in sinks, troughs, pans or scree beds.
B. The plant in question is best accommodated in a trough or sink.
C. Suitable for peat beds and the 'Billiard Table', as described in Chapter One.

Type. This is abbreviated to H for herb, H.P for herbaceous perennial, S for shrub and S.S for sub shrub, B for bulb, followed by E for evergreen, D for deciduous.

Height and Spread. The approximate height is given first, followed by the approximate spread. For example, 1 × 4 means 1 inch high and covering a space 4 inches in width when mature. Conditions of soil and aspect will affect the overall size of the plants in different localities and figures given should be used bearing these points in mind.

Soil. The figures A, B, C and D denote that the plant in question requires one of the soil mixtures described under these letters in Chapter Two (p. 36). The letters N or L denote that a neutral or limy medium is required. Where no letter is given the plant will thrive under either condition.

Position and Protection. The following terms and abbreviations used singly or in combination will minimize the risk of planting in an unsuitable spot:

S.   A shady position either facing north or protected by a rock.

H.S. A half-shady spot or facing west with protection from the south by a shadow cast by either a rock or shrub.

Sun This means that the plant will require a normal amount of direct sunlight.

C.   This means that the plant will do well planted on its side in a crevice built up on the rocks for preference.

W.   The plant will do well planted in a vertical position in the side of a trough or scree frame.

P.   This plant requires a pane of glass suspended over it in winter, generally from October to the end of March.

Colour and Season. This column is self-explanatory; for example, Red, June means that the flowers are red and the flowering season is June. A double entry such as White May means that the plant Red October has white flowers in May and red fruits or berries in October.

Propagation. Under this heading a general idea is given as to the best method of increasing the stock:

S.   The best method is by seed.

D.   Division.

G.C.   Green cuttings in late spring.

C.   Half ripened wood at the end of July.

R.C.   Fully ripened wood at the end of September.

L.   Layering.

Leaf C. The plant is best propagated by leaf cuttings.

Root C. As above, but using the thick root thongs to increase the stock.

H. Where this letter is placed after any of the above abbreviations it means that bottom heat is essential to obtain a fair percentage of strikes.

The omission of this letter does not mean that bottom heat cannot be employed; in fact, its use will certainly save an appreciable amount of time taken to increase the stock.

A combination of the above will denote that the plant can be increased by the methods which the abbreviated letters stand for: Example: SAXIFRAGA *grisebachii* S.G.C means that the plant can be increased by seed or green cuttings.

Name of Plant	Suitability	Type	Height and spread in inches	Soil	Position and Protection	Colour and Season		Propagation
ACANTHOLIMON								
androsaceum (syn. *A. echinus*)	A	S.S.E	6×6	A	Sun	White	June	C.H
creticum	,,	,,	3×4	,,	,,	,,	,,	,,
libanoticum	,,	,,	3×4	,,	,,	,,	,,	,,
olivieri	,,	,,	6×6	,,	,,	Pink	,,	,,
venustum	,,	,,	6×6	,,	,,	,,	,,	,,
AETHIONEMA								
armenum	,,	,,	4×8	,,	,,	,,	,,	G.C
kotschyi	B	,,	3×4	,,	,,	,,	,,	G.C.S
schistosum	A	,,	4×8	,,	,,	,,	,,	G.C
ALLIUM								
cyaneum	,,	B	6×3	,,	,,	Blue	July	S
narcissiflorum	,,	,,	6×3	,,	,,	Pink	Aug.	,,
platycaule (syn. *A. anceps*)	,,	,,	6×4	,,	,,	,,	,,	,,
sikkimense	,,	,,	6×3	,,	,,	Blue	July	,,
ALYSSUM								
alpestre	,,	S.E	3×6	,,	,,	Yellow	June	C
idaeum	,,	,,	2×6	,,	,,	,,	May	,,
montanum	,,	,,	3×6	,,	,,	,,	,,	,,
podolicum	See *Schivereckia podolica*							
spinosum	A	S.E	5×8	,,	,,	White	June	S.G.C
roseum	,,	,,	5×8	,,	,,	Light Pink	,,	,,
tortuosum	,,	,,	6×4	,,	,,	Yellow	May	C
wulfenianum	,,	,,	2×6	,,	,,	,,	,,	,,

Name of Plant	Suitability	Type	Height and spread in inches	Soil	Position and Protection	Colour and Season		Propagation
ANDROMEDA								
polifolia	C	S.E	6×9	C.N	S	Pink	May	G.C
compacta	,,	,,	6×9	,,	,,	,,	,,	,,
minima	,,	,,	2×6	,,	,,	,,	,,	,,
ANDROSACE								
aizoon coccinea (syn. *A. bulleyana*)	A	H.E	6×6	A	Sun	Scarlet	June	S
carnea	,,	,,	3×4	,,	,,	Pink	May	,,
brigantiaca	,,	,,	3×6	,,	,,	,,	,,	,,
halleri	,,	,,	3×6	,,	,,	,,	,,	,,
laggeri	,,	,,	2×4	,,	,,	,,	April	,,
chamaejasme	,,	,,	2×3	,,	,,	White	May	,,
charpentieri	,,	,,	1×3	,,	,,	Pink	,,	,,
chumbyi	,,	,,	2×6	,,	,,	Rose	,,	,,
ciliata	B	,,	½×3	D	Sun C.P	Rose	April	,,
cylindrica	,,	,,	2×4	,,	,,	White	,,	G.C
× *hirtella*	,,	,,	1×4	,,	,,	,,	May	,,
geraniifolia	,,	,,	6×8	,,	H.S.P	Pink	June	S.L
hedræantha	,,	,,	1×4	,,	Sun	Rose	May	,,
helvetica	,,	,,	2×3	,,	Sun C.P	White	April	,,
hirtella	,,	,,	2×4	,,	,,	,,	,,	G.C
imbricata (syn. *A. argentea*)	,,	,,	1×3	,,	H.S	,,	,,	S
lactea	A	,,	6×6	A	Sun	,,	,,	,,
mathildae	B	,,	1×4	D	Sun C.P	,,	,,	,,
pyrenaica	,,	,,	1×4	,,	,,	,,	,,	S.G.C
sempervivoides	A	,,	2×6	,,	Sun	Pink	,,	G.C
spinulifera	B	,,	6×6	,,	Sun C.P	Lilac	June	S
villosa	A	,,	2×4	A	Sun	White	April	D
arachnoidea	,,	,,	2×6	,,	,,	,,	,,	,,
ANEMONE								
alpina sulphurea	See *Pulsatilla alpina sulphurea*							
apennina	A	H.P	4×8	A	Sun	Blue	,,	D.S.
baldensis	,,	,,	3×6	,,	,,	White	May	S
blanda	,,	,,	4×8	,,	,,	Blue	April	D.S
atrocaerulea	,,	,,	4×8	,,	,,	,,	,,	,,
halleri	See *Pulsatilla halleri*							
vernalis	,, *Pulsatilla vernalis*							
ANOMATHECA	See LAPEYROUSIA							

Name of Plant	Suitability	Type	Height and spread in inches	Soil	Position and Protection	Colour and Season		Propagation

NTHYLLIS

montana	A	S.E	3×8	A	Sun	Rose	May	C
rubra	,,	,,	3×8	,,	,,	Red	,,	,,

QUILEGIA

eed is the only practical method of increasing the dwarf 'Columbine' but nfortunately all the species readily hybridize with each other so that where a umber of different plants are grown together, steps must be taken at flowering me to isolate the flowers required for seed. The majority of the species vary in eight and are best purchased as adult flowering plants so that plants of dwarf ature are obtained.

bernardii	B	H.P.	4×4	B	Sun	Blue	May	S
bertolonii	,,	,,	4×4	,,	,,	,,	,,	,,
canadensis	A	,,	6×6	,,	,,	Scarlet sepals, yellow petals	June	,,
discolor	,,	,,	6×6	,,	,,	Blue sepals, white petals	May	,,
flabellata	,,	,,	6×6	,,	,,	Blue	,,	,,
alba	,,	,,	4×6	,,	,,	White	,,	,,
nana (syn. *A. akitensis kurilensis*)	,,	,,	4×6	,,	,,	Blue	,,	,,
pumila (syn. *A. akitensis*)	,,	,,	4×6	,,	,,	Blue	,,	,,
onesii	B	,,	3×4	A	,,	Blue	June	,,
elatior	,,	,,	4×6	,,	,,	,,	,,	,,
laramiensis	,,	,,	2×3	,,	,,	Cream	May	,,
moorcroftiana	,,	,,	6×6	B	,,	Blue	,,	,,
pyrenaica	A	,,	6×6	A	H.S	,,	,,	,,
saximontana	B	,,	4×6	,,	Sun	Blue sepals, white petals	June	,,
scopulorum	,,	,,	4×6	,,	,,	Flax blue	,,	,,

RABIS

androsacea	,,	H.E	1×4	D	,,	White	,,	G.C
bryoides	,,	,,	2×4	,,	,,	,,	April	,,
olympica	,,	,,	1×3	,,	,,	,,	May	,,

Name of Plant	Suita-bility	Type	Height and spread in inches	Soil	Position and Protection	Colour and Season		Propa-gation
ARABIS (*cont.*)								
carduchorum	B	H.E	2×5	A	Sun	White	April	G.C
(syn. *Draba gigas*)								
cypria	A	,,	6×6	,,	Sun P	Pink	,,	S
ARCTERICA								
nana	C	S.E	2×8	C.N	S	White	,,	G.C.L
ARCTOSTAPHYLOS								
alpina	C	S.D	2×9	B.N	,,	White	May	G.C
						Black	Sept.	
ruber	,,	,,	2×9	,,	,,	White	May	,,
						Red	Sept.	
nevadensis	,,	S.E	3×12	,,	,,	Pinkish	May	,,
nummularia	,,	,,	8×8	,,	,,	,,	,,	,,
ARENARIA								
ledebouriana	A	H.E	4×6	A	Sun	White	,,	,,
norvegica	,,	,,	2×4	,,	,,	,,	,,	,,
tetraquetra	,,	,,	2×6	,,	Sun C	,,	June	,,
granatensis	,,	,,	1×4	,,	Sun	,,	,,	,,
verna	See *Minuartia verna*							
ARMERIA								
caespitosa	A	H.E	2×6	A	,,	Pink	May	,,
Bevan's Variety	,,	,,	2×6	,,	,,	Deep pink	,,	,,
ARTEMISIA								
glacialis	B	,,	1×6	D	,,	Silver foliage	,,	,,
mutellina	A	S.S.E	2×6	A	,,	,,	,,	,,
ASPERULA								
lilaciflora	B	H.E	½×6	,,	Sun P	Pink	June	,,
suberosa	,,	,,	2×8	,,	,,	,,	,,	,,
(syn. *A. athoa*)								
ASPHODELUS								
acaulis	,,	,,	2×4	,,	,,	,,	March	D.S
ASTILBE								
×*crispa*	A	H.P	6×8	B	Sun	Rose	July	D
glaberrima saxatilis	,,	,,	3×6	,,	,,	Rose-pink	,,	,,

Name of Plant	Suitability	Type	Height and spread in inches	Soil	Position and Protection	Colour and Season		Propagation
BYKINIA								
amesii	A	H.P	6×6	A	Sun	Cherry-red	June	D
RYANTHUS								
melinii	C	S.E	1×8	C.N	S	Rose	May	L
(syn. *B. musciformis*)								
ALCEOLARIA								
iflora	A	H.E	4×6	B	H.S	Yellow	June	S
darwinii	,,	,,	4×6	,,	,,	Gold and maroon	,,	S.D
othergillii	,,	,,	4×6	,,	,,	Yellow and red	July	S
enella	,,	,,	2×6	,,	S	Yellow	June	D
AMPANULA								

his is a genus which looks very attractive when confined to a trough where its ormal habit of spreading by runners is best controlled.

abietina	B	H.P	6×6	A	Sun	Violet	June	S
llionii	,,	,,	2×8	,,	,,	Purple	,,	D
(syn. *C. alpestris*)								
alba	,,	,,	2×6	,,	,,	White	,,	,,
Frank Barker	,,	,,	2×8	,,	,,	Pink	,,	,,
grandiflora	,,	,,	2×8	,,	,,	Purple	,,	,,
argyrotricha	,,	,,	2×6	,,	,,	Mauve	,,	S
arvatica	,,	H.E	1×6	,,	,,	Violet	,,	D
alba	,,	,,	1×6	,,	,,	White	,,	,,
aucheri	,,	,,	4×6	,,	,,	Purple	,,	S
aespitosa	,,	H.P	4×6	,,	,,	Pale blue	,,	D
enisia	,,	,,	3×6	D	,,	Steel blue	,,	S
latines	,,	H.E	3×8	A	Sun W	Violet	July	,,
xcisa	,,	H.P	3×6	,,	,,	Blue	June	D
ercegovina	,,	,,	3×6	,,	,,	Lilac-blue	July	S.G.C
kewensis (excisa × arvatica)	,,	,,	4×6	,,	,,	Pale mauve	,,	D
asiocarpa	,,	H.E	4×6	,,	,,	Pale blue	,,	S
morettiana	,,	H.P	2×6	D	Sun C	Violet-blue	,,	,,
petrophila	,,	,,	3×6	A	Sun W	Pale blue	,,	,,
ilosa	,,	H.E	4×6	,,	Sun C	Pale blue	June	,,
iperi	,,	,,	6×6	D	,,	Lilac-blue	,,	,,
aineri	,,	H.P	3×6	A	Sun	China blue	July	,,
alba	,,	,,	3×6	,,	,,	White	,,	,,

Name of Plant	Suitability	Type	Height and spread in inches	Soil	Position and Protection	Colour and Season		Propagation
CAMPANULA (*cont.*)								
saxifraga	B	H.E	4×6	A	Sun C.P	Violet	June	S
zoysii	,,	,,	2×4	D.L	Sun	Pale blue	,,	,,
CARMICHAELIA								
enysii	A	S.E	6×6	B	,,	Deep violet	,,	S.C
CASSIOPE								
fastigiata	C	,,	5×4	C.N	S	White	May	G.C
lycopodioides	,,	,,	1×8	,,	,,	,,	April	,,
major (syn. *C. rigida*)	,,	,,	2×8	,,	,,	,,	May	,,
mertensiana	,,	,,	9×6	,,	,,	,,	,,	,,
selaginoides	,,	,,	3×6	,,	,,	,,	,,	,,
stelleriana (syn. *Harrimanella stelleriana*)	,,	,,	3×6	,,	,,	White tinged pink	,,	,,
tetragona	,,	,,	9×6	,,	,,	White	,,	,,
wardii	,,	,,	6×6	,,	,,	,,	April	G.C.S
CEANOTHUS								
prostratus	A	,,	2×8	B	Sun	Blue	May	G.C
CELMISIA								
argentea	A	H.E	1×4	D	,,	White	June	S
sessiliflora	,,	,,	3×6	,,	,,	,,	,,	,,
CELSIA								
acaulis	B	,,	1×5	A	,,	Yellow	May	,,
CENTAUREA								
pindicola	,,	,,	3×6	,,	,,	Pink	,,	,,
CENTAURIUM								
scilloides	,,	,,	3×6	,,	,,	,,	April	,,
CHIONODOXA								
luciliae	A	B	4×2	,,	,,	Blue	,,	D
alba	,,	,,	4×2	,,	,,	White	,,	,,
sardensis	,,	,,	4×2	,,	,,	Deep blue	,,	,,
tmoli	,,	,,	4×2	,,	,,	Light blue	,,	,,
CONVOLVULUS								
nitidus	,,	S.S.E	1×8	,,	,,	Pink	July	G.C.H

Name of Plant	Suita-bility	Type	Height and spread in inches	Soil	Position and Protection	Colour and Season		Propa-gation
CORYDALIS								
kashmiriana	B	B	4×4	B	H.S	Blue	May	D
CRASSULA								
sarcocaulis	,,	S.D	8×6	,,	Sun P	Pink	July	G.C
mediformis	,,	H.E	3×4	,,	Sun	,,	June	,,
CROCUS								
balansae	,,	B	2×4	,,	,,	Orange	Mar.	D.S
biflorus	,,	,,	3×4	,,	,,	Buff and purple	,,	,,
chrysanthus	,,	,,	4×4	,,	,,	Golden-yellow	,,	D
E. A. Bowles	,,	,,	4×3	,,	,,	Golden	,,	,,
etruscus	,,	,,	3×4	,,	,,	Pale yellow	,,	,,
fleischeri	,,	,,	3×3	,,	,,	White	,,	D.S
imperati	,,	,,	3×3	,,	,,	Buff with purple	Feb.	D
longiflorus	,,	,,	4×3	,,	,,	Violet	Nov.	,,
medius	,,	,,	2×3	,,	,,	Purple	,,	,,
ochroleucus	,,	,,	3×3	,,	,,	White	,,	,,
pulchellus	,,	,,	3×3	,,	,,	Lavender	Oct.	,,
salzmannii	,,	,,	4×4	,,	,,	Lilac	,,	,,
sativus	,,	,,	4×4	,,	,,	Purple	,,	,,
sieberi	,,	,,	3×4	A	,,	Purple-blue	Mar.	,,
speciosus	,,	,,	3×3	,,	,,	Blue	Oct.	,,
stellaris	,,	,,	3×3	,,	,,	Orange	Mar.	,,
susianus	,,	,,	3×3	,,	,,	Gold	,,	,,
versicolor	,,	,,	3×3	,,	,,	White and violet	,,	,,
zonatus	,,	,,	4×4	,,	,,	Lavender-blue	Sept.	,,
CYANANTHUS								
delavayi	A	H.P	3×6	,,	,,	Violet-blue	July	S.G.C
formosus	,,	,,	3×6	,,	,,	Violet	Aug.	,,
lobatus	,,	,,	3×8	,,	Sun W	Blue	,,	,,
farreri	,,	,,	1×5	,,	Sun P	,,	,,	,,
longiflorus	,,	,,	3×6	,,	Sun C	Purple-blue	,,	,,
microphyllus	,,	,,	3×6	,,	Sun	Blue	,,	,,

Name of Plant	Suitability	Type	Height and spread in inches	Soil	Position and Protection	Colour and Season		Propagation
CYCLAMEN								
africanum	B	B	4×4	A.L	H.S.P	Pale pink	Oct.	S
cilicicum	,,	,,	3×4	,,	H.S	,,	Sept.	,,
coum	,,	,,	3×4	,,	,,	Magenta	Feb.	,,
album	,,	,,	3×4	,,	,,	White	,,	,,
roseum	,,	,,	3×4	,,	,,	Pink	,,	,,
europaeum	,,	,,	4×6	,,	,,	Crimson	Aug.	,,
graecum	,,	,,	4×4	,,	H.S.P	Pink	,,	,,
hiemale	,,	,,	4×4	,,	H.S	Carmine	Jan.	,,
ibericum	,,	,,	4×6	,,	,,	,,	,,	,,
libanoticum	,,	,,	6×6	,,	H.S.P	Rose-pink	March	,,
repandum	,,	,,	6×6	,,	H.S	Deep pink	April	,,
album	,,	,,	6×6	,,	,,	White	,,	,,
CYTISUS								
ardoinii	A	S.D	4×8	A	Sun	Yellow	,,	G.C
demissus (syn. *C. hirsutus demissus*)	,,	,,	3×6	,,	,,	,,	,,	G.C.S
DALIBARDA								
repens	,,	,,	3×1	C	S	White	May	G.C
DAPHNE								

DAPHNE

A fine race of plants, but not as easy as is often made out in nurserymen catalogues. All resent root disturbance once planted. They should be placed with their roots in shade and flowers in sun.

Name of Plant	Suitability	Type	Height and spread in inches	Soil	Position and Protection	Colour and Season		Propagation
arbuscula	A	S.E	6×9	B	Sun	Deep pink	May	G.C.H
oleoides	,,	,,	9×9	,,	,,	Cream	,,	S
						Orange	Aug.	G.C.H
petraea	,,	,,	4×6	,,	Sun C	Rose-pink	May	C
grandiflora	,,	,,	4×6	,,	,,	Pink	June	,,
striata	B	,,	4×6	,,	Sun	Deep pink	May	,,
alba	,,	,,	4×6	,,	,,	White	,,	,,
DIANTHUS								
callizonus	A	H.E	4×8	A	,,	Rose-pink	June	G.C
freynii	,,	,,	2×6	A.N	,,	Deep rose	,,	,,
glacialis	,,	,,	2×6	,,	,,	Deep pink	,,	,,

Name of Plant	Suitability	Type	Height and spread in inches	Soil	Position and Protection	Colour and Season		Propagation
aematocalyx	A	H.E	3×6	A.N	Sun	Purple-red	June	G.C
Highland Fraser	,,	,,	5×6	,,	,,	Pink	,,	,,
Jupiter	,,	,,	4×6	,,	,,	Salmon-pink	May	,,
La Bourbille	,,	,,	1×3	,,	,,	Pink	,,	,,
La Bourbille Alba	,,	,,	1×3	,,	,,	White	,,	,,
Mars	,,	,,	3×6	,,	,,	Crimson	June	,,
icrolepis (syn. *D. pumilus*)	,,	,,	1×6	A	,,	Pink	May	,,
eglectus	,,	,,	4×6	A.N	,,	Cherry-rose	June	,,
eanus	,,	,,	5×6	A	,,	White	,,	,,
indicola	,,	,,	2×4	,,	,,	Rose-pink	,,	,,
imulans	,,	,,	3×6	,,	,,	Deep pink	May	,,
APENSIA								
apponica	C	S.E	2×8	C.N	S	White	June	C.H
obovata	,,	,,	2×8	,,	,,	,,	,,	,,
OSPHAERA	See TRACHELIUM							
UGLASIA								
aevigata	B	H.E	2×6	A	Sun	Rose-red	May	G.C.D
aontana	,,	,,	2×6	,,	,,	Rose-pink	,,	,,
italiana	,,	,,	1×6	,,	,,	Yellow	,,	,,
praetutiana	,,	,,	1×5	,,	,,	,,	,,	,,
RABA								
caulis	,,	,,	1×4	D	Sun P	,,	April	S.G.C
ndina	,,	,,	1×3	A	Sun	,,	,,	,,
ryoides imbricata	A	,,	2×4	,,	,,	,,	,,	,,
edeana	B	,,	1×4	,,	Sun C.P	White	,,	,,
nollissima	,,	,,	2×6	,,	Sun P	Yellow	,,	,,
olytricha	,,	,,	2×4	,,	,,	,,	,,	,,
igida	,,	,,	2×6	,,	Sun	,,	,,	,,
RYAS								
ctopetala minor	A	S.E	2×6	,,	,,	White	May	C
DRAIANTHUS								
almaticus	B	H.P	3×6	,,	,,	Purple	June	S
umilio	,,	,,	2×6	,,	,,	Lavender	,,	,,

Name of Plant	Suitability	Type	Height and spread in inches	Soil	Position and Protection	Colour and Season		Propagation
EDRAIANTHUS (*cont.*)								
serpyllifolius	B	H.P	3×6	A	Sun	Violet	May	G.C
stenocalyx	,,	,,	2×6	,,	,,	Lavender	June	S
EPIGAEA								
asiatica	C	S.E	4×6	C.N	S	Pale pink	May	D.H
repens	,,	,,	4×6	,,	,,	,,	,,	,,
ERIGERON								
aureus	A	H.P	3×6	A	Sun	Golden	,,	S
compositus	,,	H.E	2×6	,,	,,	Lavender	,,	,,
leiomerus	,,	,,	4×6	,,	,,	Violet-blue	,,	S.D
trifidus	,,	,,	3×6	,,	,,	Lavender	,,	S
uniflorus	,,	,,	4×6	,,	,,	,,	,,	,,
ERINACEA								
anthyllis (syn. *E. pungens*)	,,	S.E	6×9	,,	,,	Lavender-blue	June	,,
ERINUS								
alpinus	,,	H.E	3×6	,,	Sun W	Lilac	May	,,
albus	,,	,,	3×6	,,	,,	White	,,	,,
Dr Hanele	,,	,,	3×6	,,	,,	Carmine	June	,,
Mrs C. Boyle	,,	,,	3×6	,,	,,	Pink	,,	,,
ERIOGONUM								
ovalifolium	B	,,	6×6	,,	Sun	White	,,	G.C
ERITRICHIUM								
nipponicum	,,	,,	3×4	,,	,,	Blue	,,	S
ERODIUM								
chamaedryoides (syn. *E. reichardii*)	A	,,	1×6	,,	,,	White	May	G.C
roseum	,,	,,	1×6	,,	,,	Pink	,,	,,
ERYTHRONIUM								
californicum	,,	B	6×3	B	H.S	Cream	Mar.	S
dens-canis	,,	,,	6×3	,,	,,	Rose	April	,,
hendersonii	,,	,,	6×3	,,	,,	Lavender	,,	,,
EUNOMIA								
oppositifolia	,,	H.E	2×8	A	Sun	,,	,,	,,

Lewisia pygmaea (see p. 102).

Narcissus bulbocodium romieuxii (see p. 105).

Oxalis enneaphylla minuta (see p. 131).

Phlox nana ensifolia (see p. 107).

Myosotis rupicola, an outstanding miniature forget-me-not from the European Alps (see p. 104).

Penstemon rupicola, an unusually attractive dwarf shrub from the State of Washington, U.S.A. (see p. 107).

Rhodohypoxis baurii, a hardy South African bulbous plant for a sheltered, sunny position (see p. 114).

Saxifraga × *jenkinsae*, a hybrid for early spring flowering (see p. 117).

Phyteuma comosum (see p. 108).

Platycodon grandiflorum Apoyana (see p. 132).

Polygala chamaebuxus (see p. 109).

Potentilla aurea (see p. 109).

Name of Plant	Suita-bility	Type	Height and spread in inches	Soil	Position and Protection	Colour and Season		Propa-gation
MELEA								
ostrata	A	S.E	3×9	B	Sun	White	May Aug.	G.C
oarctata	,,	,,	3×9	,,	,,	,, ,,	May Aug.	,,
LYGALA								
lcarea	B	H.E	2×8	C.L	H.S	Blue	May	S
amaebuxus	,,	S.E	4×9	C.N	,,	White and yellow	,,	G.C
urpurea (syn. *P. c. grandiflora*)	,,	,,	6×9	,,	,,	Purplish-red and yellow	,,	,,
aucifolia	,,	,,	2×9	,,	,,	Bright carmine	June	S
yredae	,,	,,	2×9	,,	,,	Purple and yellow	May	G.C
LYGONUM								
nuicaule	,,	H.P	2×5	A	,,	White	April	D
TENTILLA								
lba	A	,,	3×9	A.N	Sun	,,	,,	,,
urea	,,	,,	3×6	,,	,,	Yellow	May	S
rviseta	,,	H.E	2×3	,,	,,	Golden-yellow	,,	,,
evadensis	,,	,,	4×9	,,	,,	Yellow	June	G.C
itida	B	,,	2×6	A.L	,,	Rose	,,	D
erna nana	,,	H.P	1×6	A.N	,,	Golden	April	,,

IMULA

ere are two main sections to this vast race of plants, European and Asiatic.
e former are mostly sun lovers dwelling in open exposed rock faces while the
ter are from moist, well-drained, high alpine meadows, and prefer shade in
ltivation.

IMULA (European)								
llionii	B	H.E	2×4	A	Sun C.P	Rose-red	April	G.C.S
alba	,,	,,	2×4	,,	,,	White	,,	G.C
Ethel Barker	,,	,,	2×4	,,	,,	Deep rose	,,	,,
uricula ciliata	,,	,,	6×4	,,	Sun	Yellow	May	,,
× *berninae*	,,	,,	3×4	,,	,,	Bluish-red	,,	,,
(*rubra* × *viscosa*)								

Name of Plant	Suitability	Type	Height and spread in inches	Soil	Position and Protection	Colour and Season		Propagation
PRIMULA (European) (*cont.*)								
×*biflora* (*minima*×*glutinosa*)	B	H.E	1×3	A	Sun	Rosy-purple	May	G.C
×*bileckii* (*minima*×*rubra*)	,,	,,	1×3	,,	,,	Red	,,	,,
carniolica	,,	,,	6×4	,,	H.S	Rose	,,	G.C.
darialica	,,	,,	3×4	,,	Sun	Lavender	,,	S
farinosa	,,	H.P	2×3	,,	H.S	Pink	,,	,,
×*forsteri* (*minima*×*rubra*)	,,	H.E	1×3	,,	,,	Deep rose	,,	G.C
frondosa	,,	H.P	5×6	,,	,,	Rose	,,	S.G.
glutinosa	,,	H.E	3×3	A.N	,,	Purplish-blue	,,	,,
hirsuta	See *P. rubra*							
longiflora (syn. *P. halleri*)	,,	H.P	6×3	,,	Sun	Pink	,,	S
marginata	B	H.E	4×6	A.L	Sun C	Lavender-blue	,,	C
caerulea	,,	,,	4×6	,,	,,	Blue	,,	,,
grandiflora	,,	,,	6×6	,,	,,	Lavender-blue	,,	,,
Linda Pope	,,	,,	4×6	,,	,,	Clear lavender-blue	,,	,,
Prichard's Variety	,,	,,	4×6	,,	,,	Lavender-blue	,,	,,
rosea	,,	,,	4×6	,,	,,	Reddish-blue	,,	,,
Marven (*marginata*×*venusta*)	,,	,,	6×6	,,	Sun	Violet	,,	,,
minima	B	,,	2×4	,,	,,	Rose	,,	,,
alba	,,	,,	2×4	,,	,,	White	,,	,,
×*pubescens* (*auricula*×*rubra*)	,,	,,	4×6	,,	,,	Crimson	,,	G.C
,, *alba*	,,	,,	4×6	,,	,,	White	,,	,,
,, Faldonside	,,	,,	4×6	,,	,,	Crimson	,,	,,
,, Ladybird	,,	,,	4×6	,,	,,	Red	,,	,,
,, Mrs J. H. Wilson	,,	,,	4×6	,,	H.S	Deep lilac	,,	,,
,, Sulphur Gem	,,	,,	4×6	,,	Sun	Yellow	,,	,,
,, The General	,,	,,	4×6	,,	,,	Terra-cotta red	,,	,,

Name of Plant	Suita-bility	Type	Height and spread in inches	Soil	Position and Protection	Colour and Season		Propa-gation
rheiniana	B	H.E	3×4	A.L	Sun	Rich lavender	May	G.C
bra	,,	,,	3×4	,,	Sun C	Deep rose	,,	,,
otica	,,	H.P	2×2	A.N	Sun	Purple	April	S
rolensis	,,	H.E	3×6	A.L	,,	Magenta	June	G.C

IMULA (Asiatic)

fortunately, the majority of the Asiatic primulas suitable for cultivation in ughs and screes are not easy plants to grow and often require great skill, but this book would not be complete if these were omitted a few general hints their culture will possibly help. All require a cool, shady, north-facing sition and are best planted where rain cannot lodge on the foliage, thus ting up crown rot. Use of rock and glass as methods of protection will assist terially in cultivating these very desirable plants.

llidifolia	A	H.P	5×5	B	S.P	Purplish-blue	May	S
butanica	,,	,,	1×5	,,	,,	Blue	April	S.D
acteosa	,,	,,	2×6	,,	,,	Rose-pink	,,	,,
arkei	,,	,,	2×4	,,	,,	Deep pink	,,	D
gworthii	,,	,,	3×5	,,	,,	Pale mauve	Mar.	D.S
yn. *P. winteri*)								
alba	,,	,,	3×5	,,	,,	White	April	D
acilipes	,,	,,	1×5	,,	,,	Mauve	,,	,,
Pandora	,,	,,	2×6	,,	,,	Bright pink	Mar.	D. Leaf C
dgworthii × scapigera)								
ptans	A	,,	1×4	,,	,,	Violet	April	D
apigera	,,	,,	3×5	,,	,,	Rose-pink	,,	,,
ssilis	,,	,,	2×5	,,	,,	Purplish-pink	,,	,,
yloriana	,,	,,	4×2	,,	,,	Violet-pink	,,	S

LSATILLA (formerly ANEMONE)

pina sulphurea	A	H.P	6×6	A	Sun	Yellow	May	,,
alleri	,,	,,	6×6	,,	,,	Purple	April	,,
rnalis	,,	H.E	4×6	A.L	,,	White, with violet back	,,	,,

SCHKINIA

illoides	,,	B	4×3	A	,,	Light blue	,,	D
yn. *P. libanotica*)								

Name of Plant	Suita-bility	Type	Height and spread in inches	Soil	Position and Protection	Colour and Season		Propa-gation
RAMONDA								
myconi (syn. *R. pyrenaica*)	A	H.E	4×6	B	S.W	Lavender	May	S. Leaf
alba	,,	,,	4×6	,,	,,	White	,,	,,
rosea	,,	,,	4×6	,,	,,	Deep pink	,,	,,
nathaliae	,,	,,	4×6	,,	,,	Lavender-blue	,,	,,
serbica	,,	,,	4×6	,,	,,	,,	,,	,,
RANUNCULUS								
anemonoides	,,	H.P	4×6	A.N	Sun	White	,,	D
calandrinioides	,,	,,	4×6	,,	,,	White, flushed pink	Feb.	,,
crenatus	,,	H.E	2×4	,,	,,	White	June	S
glacialis	,,	H.P	3×4	,,	,,	White to pink	,,	D
parnassifolius	,,	,,	6×6	,,	,,	White	May	S
seguieri	,,	,,	3×4	A.L	,,	,,	June	D
RAOULIA								
australis	B	H.E	1×8	A	,,	Yellow	,,	,,
glabra	,,	,,	1×8	,,	,,	White	,,	,,
grandiflora	,,	,,	1×4	,,	,,	,,	,,	G.C
lutescens	,,	,,	1×6	,,	,,	Yellow	,,	D

RHODODENDRON

No other race of flowering plants has such a diversity of colour and form. The colours include white to cream, cream to deep yellow and even orange; lig pinks, through reds to crimson and on to magenta, purple and almost to blac such as in a good form of *R. myrtilloides*. There are even many shades of blu with only a slight trace of red in their makeup. The foliage, too, provides i quota of colours to take up the show once the floral season has passed, th providing 12 months of display in every year. They have only one fad—th need for an absolutely lime-free soil, otherwise they are not difficult to cultiva and for those whose soil contains lime the 'billiard table' method of cultivatio is ideal (see p. 27).

aperantum	C	S.E	9×12	C.N	S	White, rose or yellow	May	S.C.L
brachyanthum	,,	,,	6×12	,,	,,	Yellow	June	,,
hypolepidotum	,,	,,	9×12	,,	,,	Pale yellow	,,	,,

ABOVE LEFT: *Potentilla nitida* (see p. 109).
ABOVE RIGHT: *Primula rosea* (see p. 110).
BELOW: *Rhodohypoxis* Ruth (see p. 114).

Salix apoda (male form) (see p. 114).

Saxifraga grisebachii Wisley Variety (see p. 117).

Name of Plant	Suitability	Type	Height and spread in inches	Soil	Position and Protection	Colour and Season		Propagation
ᴋTILLARIA								
tifolia nobilis (syn. *F. messanensis*)	A	B	3×4	B	Sun	Mottled purple	May	S
dica	,,	,,	6×2	,,	,,	Yellow	April	,,
ᴜULTHERIA								
enothrix	C	S.E	9×12	C.N	H.S	White, flushed pink	June	G.C
						Red	Oct.	L.S
neata	,,	,,	9×12	,,	,,	White	June	G.C
						,,	Oct.	L.S
pressa	,,	,,	6×9	,,	,,	White	June	G.C
						Red	Oct.	L.S
ructa alba	,,	,,	6×9	,,	,,	White	June	G.C
						,,	Oct.	L.S
umifusa (syn. *G. myrsinites*)	,,	,,	2×8	,,	,,	Flushed pink	June	G.C
						Red	Oct.	L.S
iqueliana	,,	,,	4×8	,,	,,	White	June	G.C
						,,	Oct.	L.S
atifolia	,,	,,	6×9	,,	,,	Pink	June	G.C
						Scarlet	Oct.	L.S
rolifolia (syn. *G. pyroloides*)	,,	,,	4×9	,,	,,	White, flushed pink	June	G.C
						Purple	Oct.	L.S
upestris	,,	,,	6×9	,,	,,	White	June	G.C
						Scarlet	Oct.	L.S
ymifolia	,,	,,	6×9	,,	,,	White	June	G.C
						Violet	Oct.	L.S
ichophylla	,,	,,	4×9	,,	,,	Pinkish-white	June	G.C
						Blue	Sept.	L.S
ᴀYLUSSACIA								
rachycera	,,	,,	9×12	,,	,,	White, flushed pink	April	G.C
ᴇNISTA								
spalathoides (syn. *G. lobelii*)	A	S.D	3×12	A	Sun	Yellow	June	S.C

Name of Plant	Suita-bility	Type	Height and spread in inches	Soil	Position and Protection	Colour and Season		Prop gatio
GENISTA (*cont.*)								
dalmatica (syn. *G. silvestris pungens*)	A	S.D	6×9	A	Sun	Yellow	June	S.C
delphinensis (syn. *G. sagittalis minor*)	,,	,,	2×9	,,	,,	,,	,,	,,
januensis	,,	,,	3×8	,,	,,	,,	,,	,,
patula	,,	,,	3×9	,,	,,	,,	,,	,,
sylvestris procumbens	,,	,,	3×12	,,	,,	,,	July	,,
villarsii (syn. *G. pulchella*)	,,	,,	2×6	,,	,,	,,	June	,,

GENTIANA

A race of plants always in the forefront where alpines are discussed; it must admitted that they are not as easy as catalogues make out but when satisf. nothing can surpass their beauty. All benefit from a top-dressing of equal parts loam, leafmould and sand worked down among the rosettes in early spring.

alpina	A	H.E	2×6	B.N	Sun	Blue	April	D.S
altaica	,,	,,	2×6	B	Sun P	,,	May	S
cachemirica	,,	H.P	6×8	,,	H.S	,,	Aug.	,,
farreri	,,	,,	6×6	,,	,,	Light blue	,,	,,
freyniana	,,	,,	6×8	,,	Sun	Blue	July	,,
froelichii	,,	H.E	3×6	,,	,,	Pale blue	,,	,,
gilvo-striata	,,	,,	3×6	,,	,,	,,	Sept.	,,
loderi	,,	,,	3×9	,,	,,	Blue	July	,,
ornata	,,	H.P	4×8	,,	,,	,,	Aug.	S.D
pyrenaica	,,	,,	3×6	Leaf-mould	,,	,,	May	S
saxosa	,,	H.E	2×6	B.N	,,	White	July	,,
veitchiorum	,,	,,	4×6	,,	,,	Blue	June	S.D
verna	,,	,,	3×4	B	,,	,,	May	S
angulosa	,,	,,	3×4	,,	,,	,,	,,	,,
GERANIUM								
cinereum	,,	,,	4×6	A	,,	Pink	,,	,,
album	,,	,,	4×6	,,	,,	White	,,	,,
dalmaticum	,,	,,	6×6	,,	,,	Pink	June	,,
napuligerum	,,	,,	4×6	,,	,,	,,	May	,,
subcaulescens	,,	H.P	6×6	,,	,,	Rose	June	,,
wallichianum	,,	,,	6×6	,,	,,	Blue	July	,,

Name of Plant	Suitability	Type	Height and spread in inches	Soil	Position and Protection	Colour and Season		Propagation
OBULARIA								
rdifolia	A	S.E	2×6	A	Sun	Lavender	June	D.G.C
alba	,,	,,	2×6	,,	,,	White	,,	,,
bellidifolia	,,	,,	2×6	,,	,,	Blue	,,	,,
mulosa	,,	,,	1×5	,,	,,	Pale blue	,,	,,
canescens	,,	,,	3×6	,,	,,	Blue	,,	,,
na	,,	,,	1×4	,,	,,	Lavender-blue	,,	,,
inosa	,,	,,	1×4	,,	,,	Blue	,,	,,
ygia	,,	,,	1×3	,,	,,	,,	,,	,,
PSOPHILA								
etioides	B	H.D	1×6	,,	,,	White	,,	,,
caucasica	,,	,,	1×4	D	,,	,,	,,	,,
BERLEA								
rdinandi-coburgii	A	H.E	3×6	B	S.W	Lilac	May	D. Leaf C
hodopensis	,,	,,	3×6	,,	,,	Deep lilac	,,	,,
virginalis	,,	,,	3×6	,,	,,	White	,,	,,
BE								
dwillii (syn. *Veronica* dwillii)	,,	S.E	6×6	A	Sun	,,	July	G.C
uchananii (syn. *Veronica* uchananii)	,,	,,	9×9	,,	,,	,,	June	,,
nana	,,	,,	1×3	,,	,,	,,	,,	,,
liolata (syn. *Veronica* illiesiana)	,,	,,	8×6	,,	,,	,,	,,	,,
pacridea (syn. *Veronica epacridea*)	,,	,,	6×6	,,	,,	,,	,,	,,
ibbsii (syn. *Veronica gibbsii*)	,,	,,	9×6	,,	,,	,,	May	,,
avaudiana (syn. *Veronica lavaudiana*)	,,	,,	4×6	,,	,,	Rose-pink	June	,,
oganioides (syn. *Veronica loganioides*)	,,	,,	6×8	,,	,,	White	July	,,
imeleoides	,,	,,	9×9	,,	,,	Reddish-blue	,,	,,

Name of Plant	Suita-bility	Type	Height and spread in inches	Soil	Position and Protection	Colour and Season		Propa-gation
HEBE (*cont.*)								
pimeleoides minor	A	S.E	3×6	A	Sun	Violet-blue	July	G.C
pinquifolia pagei	,,	,,	9×9	,,	,,	White	June	,,
raoulii (syn. *Veronica raoulii*)	,,	,,	6×6	,,	,,	Pink	July	,,
subsimilis astonii (syn. *Veronica astonii*)	,,	,,	3×4	,,	,,	White	,,	,,
tetragona (syn. *Veronica tetragona*)	,,	,,	6×6	,,	,,	,,	June	,,
tetrasticha	,,	,,	5×5	,,	,,	,,	,,	,,
HELICHRYSUM								
confertum	B	,,	4×6	,,	,,	,,	,,	S
dealbatum	,,	H.E	6×6	,,	,,	,,	,,	,,
frigidum	,,	,,	2×6	,,	Sun P	,,	,,	S.G.C
milfordiae	,,	,,	1×6	,,	Sun	,,	,,	G.C
scutellifolium	,,	S.E	9×6	,,	,,	,,	,,	C pulle from plant n cut
selago	,,	,,	6×6	,,	Sun P	,,	,,	,,
HOUSTONIA								
caerulea	,,	H.E	3×6	,,	S	Light blue	May	D
alba	,,	,,	3×6	,,	,,	White	,,	,,
Millard's Variety	,,	,,	3×6	,,	,,	Blue	,,	,,
HYPERICUM								
anagalloides	A	,,	2×6	,,	H.S	Orange-yellow	June	G.C
cuneatum	,,	,,	3×6	,,	Sun	Yellow	,,	,,
fragile	,,	,,	2×6	,,	Sun P	,,	,,	,,
ericoides	B	S.E	2×6	,,	,,	,,	,,	,,
nummularium	A	H.P	4×8	,,	Sun	,,	July	D
repens	,,	S.S.E	1×8	,,	,,	,,	June	G.C
reptans	,,	,,	1×8	,,	,,	,,	July	,,
rhodopeum	,,	S.S.D	4×8	,,	Sun W	,,	June	,,
trichocaulon	,,	S.S.E	3×8	,,	Sun	,,	,,	,,

Name of Plant	Suita-bility	Type	Height and spread in inches	Soil	Position and Protection	Colour and Season		Propa-gation
YPSELLA								
ngiflora	A	H.P	½×5	B	H.S	White, tinged pink	June	G.C
ERIS								
ordanii	,,	S.E	2×6	A	Sun	White	May	,,
agascana	,,	,,	6×6	,,	,,	,,	,,	,,
axatilis	,,	,,	3×6	,,	,,	,,	April	,,
empervirens 'Little Gem'	,,	,,	4×6	,,	,,	,,	May	,,
aurica	,,	,,	2×6	,,	,,	,,	,,	,,
enoreana	,,	,,	4×8	,,	,,	,,	,,	,,
EX								
renata bullata	B	,,	9×6	B	,,	Foliage plant	,,	C.H
mariesii	,,	,,	8×4	,,	,,	,,	,,	,,
IS								
lanfordiae	,,	B	3×3	A	,,	Yellow	Feb.	D
istrioides	,,	,,	4×3	,,	,,	Deep blue	,,	,,
acustris	,,	H.P	5×6	,,	H.S	Blue and gold	June	,,
nellita (syn. *I. rubra-narginata*)	A	,,	4×6	B	Sun	Smoky red	May	,,
ninutoaurea	,,	,,	3×6	,,	,,	Yellow	,,	,,
umila cretica	,,	,,	2×8	,,	,,	Lavender-blue	,,	,,
ASMINUM								
arkeri	,,	S.E	6×12	A	,,	Yellow Black	June Oct.	G.C.S
ALMIOPSIS								
eachiana	C	,,	9×6	C.N	S	Rose-pink	May	C.H
ELSEYA								
niflora	B	H.E	½×5	D	Sun C	White	,,	G.C
APEYROUSIA								
ruenta (syn. *Anomatheca ruenta*)	A	B	4×3	A	Sun	Salmon-pink	Aug.	S
alba	,,	,,	4×3	,,	,,	White	,,	,,

Name of Plant	Suitability	Type	Height and spread in inches	Soil	Position and Protection	Colour and Season		Propagation
LEIOPHYLLUM								
buxifolium nanum	C	S.E	9×12	C.N	S	White	May	C
LEONTOPODIUM								
alpinum crassense	A	H.P	4×4	A.C	Sun P	,,	June	S
LEUCOGENES								
grandiceps	B	S.E	4×4	,,	H.S	,,	,,	G.C
leontopodium	,,	,,	6×4	,,	,,	,,	,,	,,
LEUCOJUM								
hiemale	,,	B	4×2	A	Sun	White green	April	D
roseum	,,	,,	3×24	,,	,,	Pale pink	Sept.	D.S
LEUCOPOGON								
fraseri	C	S.E.	3×6	C.N	S	Pinkish-white	May	G.C.L
						Reddish-yellow	Sept.	
LEWISIA								
brachycalyx	B	H.P	1×3	A.N	Sun	White	May	S
columbiana	A	H.E	4×5	,,	,,	Purple	June	,,
rosea	,,	,,	4×5	,,	,,	Rose-pink	,,	S.G.C
cotyledon	,,	,,	9×6	,,	Sun W	Salmon-pink	,,	,, Leaf C
eastwoodii	,,	,,	6×6	,,	,,	Pink	,,	,,
heckneri	,,	,,	9×6	,,	,,	Rose	,,	,,
howellii	,,	,,	9×6	,,	,,	Light pink	,,	G.C Leaf C
× Jennifer (*howellii* × *heckneri*)	,,	,,	6×12	,,	,,	Light salmon, flushed pink	May	,,
leeana	,,	,,	6×6	,,	,,	Pink	,,	,,
alba	,,	,,	6×6	,,	,,	White	,,	,,
pygmaea	B	,,	2×3	,,	Sun	Pale pink	June	S
rediviva	,,	H.P	2×4	,,	,,	,,	,,	,,
tweedyi	,,	H.E	6×8	B.N	,,	Apricot	,,	G.C Leaf C
LIMONIUM								
gougetianum	A	,,	3×5	A	,,	Mauve	July	S

Name of Plant	Suitability	Type	Height and spread in inches	Soil	Position and Protection	Colour and Season		Propagation
LINARIA								
aequitriloba	A	H.P	1×6	A.N	Sun	Lavender	June	D
alpina	,,	H.E	3×9	,,	,,	Violet and orange	,,	S
LINUM								
elegans (syn. *L. iberidifolium*)	B	S.E	4×9	,,	,,	Yellow	May	G.C
salsoloides	B	H.E	6×9	,,	,,	White, veined lilac	June	,,
nanum	,,	,,	3×9	,,	,,	White	,,	,,
tenuifolium	,,	,,	2×8	,,	,,	Pink	,,	S
LITHOSPERMUM								
oleifolium	,,	S.E	6×8	A.C	,,	Light blue	May	C
LYSIMACHIA								
japonica minutissima	A	H.E	1×6	A.N	H.S	Yellow	July	D
MELANDRIUM								
This genus is often found under SILENE in catalogues.								
elisabethae	B	H.E	6×6	A	Sun	Magenta and rose	,,	S
hookeri	,,	H.P	3×6	,,	,,	Salmon-pink	,,	,,
ingramii	,,	,,	3×6	,,	,,	Rose-pink	,,	,,
MERTENSIA								
echioides	A	,,	8×6	,,	H.S	Deep blue	June	D.S
maritima	,,	,,	2×4	,,	Sun	Pale blue	July	S
primuloides	,,	,,	3×6	,,	H.S	Violet	,,	D
MICROMERIA								
graeca	B	S.E	4×6	,,	Sun	Pink	,,	C
piperella	,,	,,	6×6	,,	,,	Bright pink	,,	,,
MINUARTIA								
aretioides	,,	H.E	2×5	,,	,,	White	April	G.C
imbricata	,,	,,	2×4	,,	,,	,,	,,	,,
leucocephala	,,	,,	2×6	,,	,,	,,	,,	,,
rupestris	,,	,,	2×6	,,	,,	Pink	,,	,,

Name of Plant	Suita-bility	Type	Height and spread in inches	Soil	Position and Protection	Colour and Season		Propa-gation

MINUARTIA (*cont.*)

Name of Plant	Suita-bility	Type	Height and spread in inches	Soil	Position and Protection	Colour and Season		Propa-gation
saxifraga	B	H.E	2×6	A	Sun	White	May	G.C
verna	,,	,,	1×4	,,	,,	,,	April	,,
(syn. *Arenaria verna*)								

MITCHELLA

Name of Plant	Suita-bility	Type	Height and spread in inches	Soil	Position and Protection	Colour and Season		Propa-gation
repens	C	S.E	2×12	C.N	S	White, flushed red	June	,,
						Scarlet	Oct.	
leucocarpa	,,	,,	2×12	,,	,,	White, flushed red	June	,,
						White	Oct.	
undulata	,,	,,	2×8	,,	,,	Pink	June	,,
						Red	Oct.	

MORISIA

Name of Plant	Suita-bility	Type	Height and spread in inches	Soil	Position and Protection	Colour and Season		Propa-gation
monantha (syn. *M. hypogaea*)	B	H.E	1×4	D or A	,,	Yellow	May	Root C

MUSCARI

The bulbs will do well planted in small troughs or pans for indoor decoration many are fragrant.

Name of Plant	Suita-bility	Type	Height and spread in inches	Soil	Position and Protection	Colour and Season		Propa-gation
azureum	B	B	3×2	B	Sun	Blue	March	D.S
(syn. *Hyacinthus azureus*)								
botryoides	B	,,	4×6	,,	,,	Dark blue	,,	,,
album	,,	,,	4×6	,,	,,	White	,,	D
latifolium	,,	,,	6×3	,,	,,	Dark to light blue	April	D.S
macrocarpum (syn. *M. moschatum*)	,,	,,	6×3	,,	,,	Brownish-purple	,,	,,
flavum	,,	,,	6×3	,,	,,	Purple to yellow	,,	,,
major	,,	,,	6×3	,,	,,	Purple to pale yellow	,,	,,
neglectum	,,	,,	4×2	,,	,,	Purplish-black	,,	,,

MYOSOTIS

Name of Plant	Suita-bility	Type	Height and spread in inches	Soil	Position and Protection	Colour and Season		Propa-gation
explanata	,,	H.E	2×6	A	H.S	White	July	,,
rupicola	,,	H.P	3×4	,,	Sun	Blue	May	S
uniflora	,,	H.E	2×4	,,	,,	Yellow	June	,,

Name of Plant	Suitability	Type	Height and spread in inches	Soil	Position and Protection	Colour and Season		Propagation

MYRTUS

Name of Plant	Suitability	Type	Height and spread in inches	Soil	Position and Protection	Colour	Season	Propagation
nummularia	C	S.E	3×8	C.N	Sun P	White Pink	June Sept.	G.C

NARCISSUS

The dwarf bulbs of this genus can be grown in small troughs or pans for indoor decoration.

Name of Plant	Suitability	Type	Height and spread in inches	Soil	Position and Protection	Colour	Season	Propagation
asturiensis (syn. *N. minimus*)	B	B	3×2	B	Sun	Yellow	April	S.D
bulbocodium	,,	,,	6×3	,,	,,	,,	,,	,,
citrinus	,,	,,	6×3	,,	,,	Pale yellow	,,	D
corbularia	,,	,,	6×3	,,	,,	Yellow	,,	,,
monophyllus	,,	,,	4×3	,,	,,	Cream	Mar.	,,
romieuxii	,,	,,	3×3	,,	,,	Golden-cream	Jan.	,,
tenuifolius	,,	,,	4×2	,,	,,	Yellow	,,	,,
cernuus (syn. *N. moschatus*)	,,	,,	6×3	,,	,,	White	April	S.D
cyclamineus	,,	,,	4×2	,,	H.S	Yellow	,,	,,
juncifolius	,,	,,	3×2	,,	Sun	,,	,,	,,
rupicola	,,	,,	3×2	,,	,,	Golden-yellow	,,	,,
bulbularis (syn. *N. nanus*)	,,	,,	5×2	,,	,,	Yellow	,,	,,
marvieri	,,	,,	4×2	,,	,,	,,	,,	,,
minor	,,	,,	6×3	,,	,,	Deep yellow	,,	,,
pallidus praecox	,,	,,	6×3	,,	,,	Pale yellow	,,	,,
scaberulus	,,	,,	5×3	,,	,,	Deep yellow	,,	,,
serotinus	,,	,,	4×2	B.N	,,	Yellow and white	Oct.	,,
triandrus	,,	,,	6×3	B	H.S	Cream	April	,,
albus	,,	,,	6×3	,,	,,	White	,,	,,
calathinus	,,	,,	5×2	,,	Sun	Cream or yellow	,,	,,
concolor	,,	,,	6×3	,,	H.S	Primrose	,,	,,
pulchellus	,,	,,	6×3	,,	,,	Pale yellow	,,	,,
watieri	,,	,,	4×3	,,	Sun	White	,,	,,

Name of Plant	Suita-bility	Type	Height and spread in inches	Soil	Position and Protection	Colour and Season		Propagation
OMPHALODES								
luciliae	B	H.E	6×8	A.L	Sun	China blue	May	S
ORIGANUM								
amanum	A	S.S.E	4×8	A	Sun P	Purple and pink	July	G.C
pulchrum	,,	,,	6×8	,,	Sun	Mauve and light purple	,,	,,
ORPHANIDESIA								
gaultherioides	C	,,	6×9	C.N	S	Rose-pink	April	L.S
OXALIS								
adenophylla	B	B	3×6	A	Sun	Rosy-mauve	May	D
bowieana	,,	,,	6×8	,,	,,	Reddish-purple	,,	,,
brasiliensis	,,	,,	3×8	,,	,,	Wine red	,,	,,
chrysantha	,,	,,	2×12	,,	,,	Gold	June	,,
deppei	A	,,	6×9	,,	,,	Reddish-brown	May	,,
enneaphylla	B	,,	3×9	,,	,,	White	,,	,,
rosea	,,	,,	3×9	,,	,,	Pink	,,	,,
lobata	,,	,,	3×6	,,	,,	Gold	Sept.	,,
luteola	,,	,,	4×6	,,	,,	Deep yellow	June	,,
magellanica	,,	H.P	2×6	,,	,,	White	May	,,
oregana	,,	,,	3×8	,,	,,	Red	,,	,,
valdiviensis	,,	B	6×6	,,	,,	Yellow	Aug.	,,
PAEDEROTA								
bonarota	A	H.P	4×6	,,	H.S	Opal blue	May	S
PAPAVER								
alpinum	,,	,,	6×6	,,	Sun	White, yellow, red	June	,,
PASSERINA								
nivalis	,,	S.S.E	6×8	,,	,,	Bright yellow	Mar.	C

Name of Plant	Suitability	Type	Height and spread in inches	Soil	Position and Protection	Colour and Season		Propagation
NSTEMON								
espitosus	B	H.E	3×8	A	Sun P	Lilac-purple	June	G.C
avidsonii	,,	S.E	3×8	,,	Sun	Lilac	,,	G.C.S
enziesii	,,	S.D	6×9	,,	,,	Violet-blue	,,	G.C
icranthus	,,	S.E	4×9	,,	,,	Purple-blue	,,	,,
icrophyllus	,,	S.D	3×9	,,	,,	Violet-blue	,,	,,
inifolius	,,	S.E	·3×8	,,	,,	Red-orange	,,	G.C.S
upicola	,,	,,	4×8	,,	,,	Crimson-red	,,	C
NTACHONDRA								
umila	C	,,	6×8	C.N	S	White Red	May Sept.	G.C.H
RNETTYA								
asmanica	,,	,,	2×8	,,	,,	White Red	May Sept.	L.G.C
TROCALLIS								
yrenaica	B	H.E	2×5	D	Sun C	Lavender	May	G.C
TROPHYTUM								
aespitosum (syn. *Spiraea aespitosa*)	,,	S.S.E	1×6	A	,,	White	July	,,
endersonii (syn. *Spiraea hendersonii*)	,,	,,	3×6	,,	,,	,,	,,	,,
ILOX								
ryoides	B	S.E	1×6	D	,,	,,	May	,,
ondensata	,,	H.E	6×6	B	Sun	,,	,,	S
ouglasii	,,	,,	2×8	,,	,,	Lilac	,,	G.C
alba	,,	,,	2×8	,,	,,	White	,,	,,
Boothman's Variety	,,	,,	2×8	,,	,,	Mauve	,,	,,
Eva	,,	,,	2×8	,,	,,	Pink	,,	,,
Snow Queen	,,	,,	2×8	,,	,,	White	,,	,,
ana ensifolia (syn. *P. mesoleuca*)	A	S.D	6×9	,,	,,	Pink	,,	Root C G.C.H

Name of Plant	Suita-bility	Type	Height and spread in inches	Soil	Position and Protection	Colour and Season	Propa-gation
PHLOX (*cont.*)							
subulata	The many varieties of this species are all easy plants b possibly too rampant for our purpose. They can be us as wall plants and kept in check by being cut hard ba after flowering.						
atropurpurea	A	H.E	4×18	A	Sun	Reddish-purple	June	G.C
alicas	,,	,,	4×18	,,	,,	Pale mauve	,,	,,
Betty	,,	,,	4×18	,,	,,	Pink	,,	,,
Eventide	,,	,,	4×18	,,	,,	White, flushed lilac	,,	,,
Fairy	,,	,,	4×18	,,	,,	Lilac	,,	,,
Margery	,,	,,	4×18	,,	,,	Pink	,,	,,
Model	,,	,,	4×18	,,	,,	Lavender	,,	,,
Samson	,,	,,	4×18	,,	,,	Rose	,,	,,
Vivid	,,	,,	4×18	,,	,,	Pink	,,	,,
PHYLLODOCE							
aleutica	C	S.E	9×9	C.N	S	Yellow	May	G.C.I
breweri	,,	,,	9×9	,,	,,	Reddish-blue	,,	,,
caerulea	,,	,,	4×9	,,	,,	Reddish-purple	,,	,,
empetriformis	,,	,,	9×9	,,	,,	Red-blue	,,	,,
glanduliflora	,,	,,	6×9	,,	,,	Yellow	,,	,,
×*intermedia*	,,	,,	9×9	,,	,,	Rose-pink	,,	,,
nipponica	,,	,,	6×9	,,	,,	White	,,	,,
tsugifolia	,,	,,	12×6	,,	,,	White, flushed pink	,,	,,
PHYTEUMA							
comosum	A	H.P	3×6	A.L	Sun	Lilac	June	S
album	,,	,,	3×6	,,	,,	White	,,	,,
halleri	,,	,,	6×6	A.N	,,	Dark violet	May	,,
hedraianthifolium	,,	,,	3×6	,,	,,	Blue	June	,,
hemisphaericum	,,	,,	3×6	,,	,,	Lilac-blue	,,	,,
humile	,,	,,	3×6	,,	,,	Blue	,,	,,
pauciflorum	,,	,,	2×6	,,	,,	Blue	,,	,,
sieberi	,,	,,	6×6	,,	,,	Deep blue	,,	,,

Name of Plant	Suitability	Type	Height and spread in inches	Soil	Position and Protection	Colour and Season		Propagation
alciphilum	C	S.E	6×12	C.N	S	Rose-purple	May	S.C.L
alostrotum	,,	,,	9×12	,,	,,	Rose to purple	,,	,,
ampylogynum	,,	,,	12×12	,,	,,	Rose to purplish-black	,,	,,
amtschaticum	,,	S.D	3×12	,,	,,	Rose to crimson	,,	,,
ephalanthum crebreflorum (syn. R. crebreflorum)	,,	S.E	9×12	,,	,,	Rose-pink	,,	,,
hameunum	,,	,,	6×12	,,	,,	Purple	June	,,
haritopes	,,	,,	12×12	,,	,,	Apple pink	May	S.C
hryseum	,,	,,	12×12	,,	,,	Yellow	April	,,
osmetum	,,	,,	4×12	,,	,,	Light purple	May	S.C.L
orrestii repens	,,	,,	3×12	,,	,,	Crimson	April	,,
anceanum nanum	,,	,,	6×12	,,	,,	Yellow	June	,,
erpesticum	,,	,,	12×12	,,	,,	Orange-red	May	S.C
mpeditum	,,	,,	2×9	,,	,,	Lavender	April	S.C.L
mperator	,,	,,	3×9	,,	,,	Pale purple	May	,,
ntricatum	,,	,,	12×12	,,	,,	Mauve	April	,,
keiskei	,,	,,	4×12	,,	,,	Yellow	,,	,,
keleticum	,,	,,	4×12	,,	,,	Crimson to purple	May	,,
epidotum	,,	,,	12×12	,,	,,	Pink to purple	June	,,
itangense	,,	,,	12×12	,,	,,	Purplish-blue	May	S.C
negeratum	,,	,,	12×12	,,	S.P	Yellow	April	,,
microleucum	,,	,,	12×12	,,	S	White	May	,,
myrtilloides	,,	,,	6×12	,,	,,	Deep plum	,,	S.C.L
nitens	,,	,,	6×9	,,	,,	Magenta	July	,,
ivale	,,	,,	6×6	,,	,,	,,	May	,,
rostratum	,,	,,	4×9	,,	,,	Rose-violet	April	,,
umilum	,,	,,	6×9	,,	,,	Rose-pink	,,	,,

Name of Plant	Suita-bility	Type	Height and spread in inches	Soil	Position and Protection	Colour and Season		Propa-gation
RHODODENRON (*cont.*)								
radicans	C	S.E	1×9	C.N	S	Deep purple	May	S.C.L
rupicola	,,	,,	9×9	,,	,,	Purple	,,	S.C
sargentianum	,,	,,	12×12	,,	,,	Yellow	,,	,,
setosum	,,	,,	6×6	,,	,,	Purplish-pink	,,	,,
tapetiforme	,,	,,	3×9	,,	,,	Pink to mauve	April	S.C.L
uniflorum	,,	,,	4×9	,,	,,	Purple	,,	,,
williamsianum	,,	,,	6×24	,,	,,	Shell pink	,,	,,
RHODOHYPOXIS								
baurii	B	B	3×4	B.N	Sun	Carmine-rose	May	D.S
platypetala	,,	,,	3×4	,,	,,	White or pink	,,	,,
Eva	,,	,,	3×4	,,	,,	Deep red	,,	D
Margaret Rose	,,	,,	3×4	,,	,,	Bright pink	,,	,,
Ruth	,,	,,	3×4	,,	,,	White	,,	,,
RHODOTHAMNUS								
chamaecistus	C	S.E	9×6	C.N	S	Bright Rose	April	S.D
ROSA								
chinensis minima (syn. *R. lawranceana* and *R. roulettii*)	A	S.D	6×6	A	Sun	Crimson or pink	May	G.C
gallica pumila	,,	,,	4×6	,,	,,	Red (single)	,,	,,
×Peon	,,	,,	6×6	,,	,,	Crimson	,,	,,
RYDBERGIA								
grandiflora	,,	H.P	6×6	,,	,,	Orange	June	S
SALIX								
apoda (male form)	,,	S.D	1×8	,,	,,	Rose-pink	April	R.C
arbuscula	,,	,,	4×6	,,	,,	Yellow	,,	,,
humilis	,,	,,	2×6	,,	,,	,,	,,	,,
×*boydii*	,,	,,	6×4	,,	,,	Light yellow	,,	,,

Name of Plant	Suita-bility	Type	Height and spread in inches	Soil	Position and Protection	Colour and Season		Propa-gation
herbacea	A	S.D	2×6	A	Sun	Yellow	April	R.C
reticulata	,,	,,	3×6	,,	,,	,,	May	,,
retusa	,,	,,	2×8	,,	,,	,,	,,	,,
serpyllifolia	,,	,,	1×8	,,	,,	,,	,,	,,
SANGUINARIA								
canadensis	C	H.P	6×6	C.N	S	White	,,	S.D
flore pleno	,,	,,	6×6	,,	,,	,,	,,	,,
SAPONARIA								
×boissieri	B	H.E	3×8	A	Sun	Pink	,,	G.C
caespitosa	,,	,,	2×6	D	,,	Pale pink	,,	,,
cypria	,,	,,	3×8	A	,,	Bright pink	,,	,,
ocymoides rubra compacta	,,	,,	1×6	,,	,,	Carmine	,,	,,

SAXIFRAGA

There is no other genus of alpine plants which is more suitable for troughs or scree gardening. Small, compact and, with the exception of the 'mossy' types, never invasive, they are attractive both in or out of flower.

Name of Plant	Suita-bility	Type	Height and spread in inches	Soil	Position and Protection	Colour and Season		Propa-gation
×Ada	A	H.E	2×5	A.L	H.S	White	April May	G.C
×affinis	,,	,,	1×3	,,	,,	,,	May	,,
aizoon correvoniana	B	,,	½×3	,,	Sun C	,,	,,	,,
hirsuta	A	,,	6×5	,,	Sun	,, spotted red	,,	,,
hirtifolia	,,	,,	3×5	,,	,,	Creamy-white	,,	,,
lagraveana	,,	,,	2×6	,,	,,	White	,,	,,
minor	,,	,,	3×6	,,	,,	Creamy-white	,,	,,
minutifolia (syn. *S. baldensis*)	,,	,,	2×6	,,	,,	Creamy-white	,,	,,
venetia	,,	,,	1×6	,,	,,	White	,,	,,
×allenii	,,	,,	1×6	,,	H.S	Yellow	April	,,
×Amitie	,,	,,	1½×8	,,	,,	Lilac	,,	,,
×Arco Valleyi	B	,,	1×5	,,	,,	Rose	,,	,,
aretioides	,,	,,	2×4	,,	H.S.C	Yellow	May	,,
×assimilis	,,	,,	1½×4	,,	H.S	White	April	,,
×Bellisant	A	,,	1½×4	,,	,,	Rose-pink	,,	,,
×bertolonii	B	,,	6×4	,,	,,	Purple	,,	,,

Name of Plant	Suitability	Type	Height and spread in inches	Soil	Position and Protection	Colour and Season		Propagation

SAXIFRAGA (cont.)

Name of Plant	Suitability	Type	Height and spread in inches	Soil	Position and Protection	Colour	Season	Propagation
×*biasolettii*	B	H.E	4×6	A.L	H.S	Red	April	G.C
×*biegleri*	,,	,,	2×6	,,	,,	White	,,	,,
×*bilekii*	,,	,,	1×4	,,	H.S.C	Yellow	,,	,,
×*borisii*	A	,,	2×6	,,	H.S	,,	,,	,,
boryi	,,	,,	2×6	,,	,,	White	,,	,,
×*boydii*	B	,,	3×5	,,	,,	Yellow	,,	,,
×*burnatii*	A	,,	4×6	,,	Sun C	White	June	,,
burseriana	,,	,,	2×6	,,	H.S	,,	May	,,
Brookside	,,	,,	2×6	,,	,,	,,	,,	,,
crenata	,,	,,	1×6	,,	,,	,,	April	,,
Gloria	,,	,,	4×6	,,	,,	,,	,,	,,
His Majesty	,,	,,	3×6	,,	,,	Light pink	,,	,,
minor	B	,,	1×4	,,	H.S.C	White	,,	,,
sulphurea	A	,,	2×6	,,	H.S	Yellow	,,	,,
tridentina (syn. *S. tridentata*)	,,	,,	3×6	,,	,,	White	,,	,,
×Buttercup	,,	,,	3×6	,,	,,	Yellow	,,	,,
caesia	B	,,	2×4	,,	H.S.C	White	May	,,
cartilaginea	A	,,	6×6	,,	Sun	,,	June	,,
minor	,,	,,	3×6	,,	Sun C	,,	,,	,,
×Cecil Davis	,,	,,	3×6	,,	Sun	,,	,,	,,
×Cerise Queen (syn. S. Christine)	,,	,,	1×4	,,	H.S	Cerise	April	,,
×Cherry Trees	B	,,	2×4	,,	H.S.C	Yellow	,,	,,
cochlearis	A	,,	6×8	,,	Sun	White	June	,,
minor	,,	,,	2×5	,,	Sun C	,,	,,	,,
cotyledon	B	,,	24×12	,,	Sun	White, spotted red	,,	,,

Saxifraga cotyledon and its forms *caterhamensis, icelandica, linguaeformis, norvegica pauciflora* and *pyramidalis* if grown should be confined to a trough or sink on their own where in due season they will give an outstanding display.

Name of Plant	Suitability	Type	Height and spread in inches	Soil	Position and Protection	Colour	Season	Propagation
×Delia	A	H.E	2×6	A.L	H.S	Lilac	April	G.C
diapensioides	B	,,	1½×4	,,	Sun C	White	May	,,
lutea	,,	,,	1½×4	,,	,,	Yellow	,,	,,
×Elysium	,,	,,	1×4	,,	H.S	Rose-pink	April	,,
×Etheline	,,	,,	1×4	,,	,,	White	,,	,,
×Eudoxiana	A	,,	2×6	,,	,,	Yellow	May	,,
×Faldonside	,,	,,	2×6	,,	,,	,,	April	,,

Name of Plant	Suita-bility	Type	Height and spread in inches	Soil	Position and Protection	Colour and Season		Propa-gation
×Francis Cade	A	H.E	9×9	A.L	Sun	White	June	G.C
×Gem	B	,,	1×4	,,	H.S	Pink	April	,,
×Gloriosa	,,	,,	1×4	,,	,,	Red	,,	,,
grisebachii	,,	,,	9×6	,,	H.S.P	Pink	,,	S.G.C
Wisley Variety	,,	,,	9×6	,,	,,	,,	,,	,,
×gusmusii	,,	,,	4×6	,,	H.S	Orange	,,	G.C
×haagii	A	,,	3×8	,,	,,	Yellow	,,	,,
×Harry Marshall	,,	,,	2×6	,,	,,	Pink	,,	,,
×Iris Prichard	,,	,,	2×6	,,	,,	Brownish-red	May	,,
×irvingii	,,	,,	1×4	,,	,,	Lilac	April	,,
×jenkinsae	,,	,,	2×6	,,	,,	,,	,,	,,
juniperifolia	B	,,	2×6	,,	,,	Yellow	May	,,
×Kathleen Pinsent	A	,,	9×6	,,	Sun	Pink	June	,,
×kellereri	B	,,	3×6	,,	H.S.P	,,	Mar.	,,
×kewensis	A	,,	3×6	,,	H.S	Lilac	April	,,
kotschyi	B	,,	2×5	,,	H.S.C	Yellow	,,	,,
laevis	A	,,	1×4	,,	H.S	,,	May	,,
×landaueri	,,	,,	2×6	,,	,,	Pink	,,	,,
×Laurent Ward	,,	,,	2×6	,,	,,	Red	April	,,
×leyboldii	B	,,	2×5	,,	H.S.C	White	May	,,
lilacina	,,	,,	½×4	L.N	H.S	Lilac	April	,,
lingulata	,,	,,	24×12	A.L	Sun W	White	June	,,

Saxifraga lingulata (S. callosa) and its forms are best by themselves or planted with *S. cotyledon*. They can be used as specimens by planting them in a hole made in the side of the trough. The best forms of this species are *S. l. albida, australis, bellardii, lantoscana* (syn. *S. lantoscana*), *lantoscana superba*.

Name of Plant	Suita-bility	Type	Height and spread in inches	Soil	Position and Protection	Colour and Season		Propa-gation
longifolia	A	H.E	24×12	A.L	Sun W	White	June	S
×cotyledon	,,	,,	24×12	,,	,,	,,	,,	G.C
Tumbling Waters	,,	,,	24×12	,,	,,	,,	,,	,,
marginata	,,	,,	2×4	,,	H.S	,,	April	,,
coriophylla	B	,,	1×3	,,	H.S.C	,,	,,	,,
karadzicensis	,,	,,	1×3	,,	,,	,,	June	,,
rocheliana	,,	,,	1×3	,,	,,	,,	May	,,
purpurea	,,	,,	1½×4	,,	H.S	Buds red, white	,,	,,
mariae-theresiae	,,	,,	3×4	,,	,,	Purple	April	,,
media	,,	,,	4×6	,,	,,	Pink	,,	,,
×megasaeflora	,,	,,	2×4	,,	H.S.C	Rose	,,	,,

Name of Plant	Suita-bility	Type	Height and spread in inches	Soil	Position and Protection	Colour and	Season	Propa-gation
SAXIFRAGA (*cont.*)								
×Myra	A	H.E	1×4	A.L	H.S	Red	April	G.C
×*obristii*	,,	,,	2×6	,,	,,	White	,,	,,
oppositifolia	,,	,,	1×9	,,	S	Purplish-red	May	G.C.S
alba	,,	,,	1×6	,,	H.S	White	,,	G.C
blepharophylla	,,	,,	1×6	A.N	,,	Purplish-red	,,	,,
coccinea	,,	,,	1×8	A.L	,,	Red	,,	,,
latina	,,	,,	1×6	,,	,,	Purplish-red	,,	,,
W. A. Clark	,,	,,	1×6	,,	,,	Purple	,,	,,
Wetterhorn Variety	,,	,,	1×6	,,	,,	Red	,,	,,
×*paulinae*	,,	,,	2×6	,,	,,	Yellow	April	,,
×*petraschii*	,,	,,	2×6	,,	,,	White	,,	,,
porophylla	B	,,	4×4	,,	H.S.C.P	Pink	,,	G.C.S
montenegrina	,,	,,	4×4	,,	,,	,,	,,	,,
Okol form	,,	,,	4×4	,,	,,	Purple	,,	,,
thessalica	,,	,,	4×4	,,	,,	Pink	,,	,,
pravislavia	,,	,,	2×4	,,	H.S	Yellow	May	G.C
×Primulaize	,,	,,	2×4	,,	S	Red	June	,,
×Priory Jewel	,,	,,	1×3	,,	H.S.C	Pink	April	,,
×*prosenii*	A	,,	2×6	,,	H.S	Orange	May	,,
×*pungens*	B	,,	2×6	,,	H.S.C	Yellow	,,	,,
retusa	A	,,	½×6	,,	H.S	Red	,,	,,
×Riverslea	,,	,,	1×6	,,	,,	Rose	April	,,
×*rosinae*	,,	,,	1×6	,,	,,	White	,,	,,
×*rubella*	,,	,,	1×6	,,	,,	Pink	May	,,
sancta	B	,,	2×6	,,	H.S.C	Yellow	April	,,
scardica	,,	,,	3×6	,,	,,	White	,,	,,
obtusa	,,	,,	2×5	,,	,,	,,	,,	,,
schelleri	A	,,	1×4	,,	H.S	,,	,,	,,
×*schleicheri*	,,	,,	2×5	,,	,,	Pink	,,	,,
×*schreineri*	,,	,,	2×6	,,	,,	White	May	,,
scleropoda	,,	,,	2×4	,,	,,	Yellow	,,	,,
×Simplicity	,,	,,	1×4	,,	,,	White	April	,,
×Sonia Prichard	,,	,,	2×4	,,	,,	Purple	,,	,,
spruneri	,,	,,	2×8	,,	H.S.P	White	May	,,
squarrosa	,,	,,	2×4	,,	H.S.C	,,	,,	,,

Name of Plant	Suitability	Type	Height and spread in inches	Soil	Position and Protection	Colour and Season		Propagation
tribrnyi	A	H.E	3×3	A.L	H.S	Pink	May	G.C
zollikoferi	,,	,,	3×3	,,	,,	,,	,,	,,
×*suendermannii*	,,	,,	2×5	,,	,,	Rose	,,	,,
×*suendermannii major*	,,	,,	2×5	,,	,,	,,	,,	,,
×*suendermannii purpurea*	,,	,,	2×5	,,	,,	,,	,,	,,
×*tiroliensis*	,,	,,	1½×4	,,	H.S.C	White	,,	,,
ombeanensis	,,	,,	2×6	,,	H.S	,,	June	,,
valdensis	,,	,,	½×3	,,	,,	,,	,,	,,
andellii	B	,,	2×3	,,	H.S.C.P	,,	May	,,

CHIVERECKIA

podolica	,,	S.S.E	2×4	A	Sun	,,	,,	,,

(syn. *Alyssum podolicum*)

CHIZOCODON

soldanelloides	C	,,	4×8	C.N	S	Deep rose	April	D.S
alpinus	,,	,,	1×6	,,	,,	,,	,,	D
ilicifolius	,,	,,	3×6	,,	,,	Rose-pink	,,	D.S
albus	,,	,,	3×6	,,	,,	White	,,	D
magnus	,,	,,	2×8	,,	,,	Rose-pink	,,	,,

(syn. *S. macrophyllus*)

CILLA

autumnalis	A	B	4×2	B	Sun	Rose	Sept.	D.S
bifolia	,,	,,	4×2	,,	,,	Blue	Mar.	,,
sibirica	,,	,,	4×2	,,	,,	,,	,,	,,
verna	,,	,,	4×2	,,	,,	Light blue	,,	,,

EDUM

This is a race of plants which must be used with care in small troughs for a number are very rampant; although normally they are easy to remove, every small fleshy leaf left behind is a potential new plant. You have been warned. Flowers can generally be ignored for it is the foliage which provides the colour.

anglicum	A	H.E	3×6	A	Sun	White	June	D
brevifolium	,,	,,	1×4	,,	,,	,,	,,	,,
dasyphyllum	,,	,,	2×6	,,	,,	Pinkish	,,	,,
glanduliferum	,,	,,	2×6	,,	,,	Pink	,,	,,
macrophyllum	,,	,,	2×6	,,	,,	,,	,,	,,

Name of Plant	Suitability	Type	Height and spread in inches	Soil	Position and Protection	Colour and Season		Propagation

SEDUM (*cont.*)

Name of Plant	Suitability	Type	Height and spread in inches	Soil	Position and Protection	Colour and Season		Propagation
hispanicum aureum	A	Annual	2×6	A	Sun	Pink	June	D
minus	,,	,,	1×6	,,	,,	,,	,,	,,
hobsonii	,,	H.P	1×4	,,	,,	,,	,,	D.S
lydium	,,	H.E	1×6	A	,,	White	,,	,,
multiceps	,,	S.D	6×6	,,	,,	Yellow	,,	G.C.S
nevii	,,	H.E	3×6	,,	,,	White	,,	D
pilosum	,,	Biennial	2×6	,,	Sun C	Pink	May	S
primuloides	,,	S.D	3×6	,,	Sun	White	Aug.	C
reflexum cristatum	,,	H.E	3×6	,,	,,	—	—	,,
sempervivoides	,,	,,	6×4	,,	,,	Crimson	May	S
spathulifolium	,,	,,	3×6	,,	,,	Yellow	June	D
Capablanca	,,	,,	2×6	,,	,,	,,	,,	,,
purpureum	,,	,,	3×6	,,	,,	Golden	,,	,,
spinosum	,,	,,	4×6	,,	,,	Cream	July	,,

SEMPERVIVUM

Nothing is more charming and attractive than troughs and sinks devoted solel[y] to members of this large race. These plants are ideal for the busy gardener, eas[y] of culture, only requiring the minimum of soil and attention, in fact starvatio[n] not only restricts growth but improves the colour. They have one failing, if i[t] can be called such; that is their flowers are seldom beautiful, normally being carried on a stem which is out of proportion to the rest of the plant. Then the rosette dies after flowering, leaving a gap, so to remedy this I always remove th[e] flowering rosettes in early spring, then this gap is quickly filled by offsets. The flowers are ignored in the list, only coloration of foliage being given; the second colour given is that of the tips of the leaves.

Name of Plant	Suitability	Type	Height and spread in inches	Soil	Position and Protection	Colour and Season		Propagation
allionii	B	H.E	1×6	A	Sun	Pale green, reddish	Spring	G.C
andreanum	,,	,,	2×8	,,	,,	Bright green, brown	,,	,,
arachnoideum	,,	,,	1×6	,,	,,	Green, white	,,	,,
glabrescens	,,	,,	1×6	,,	,,	Light green, white	,,	,,
tomentosum	,,	,,	1×6	,,	,,	Green, white	,,	,,

Name of Plant	Suita-bility	Type	Height and spread in inches	Soil	Position and Protection	Colour and Season		Propa-gation
arenarium	B	H.E	$\frac{1}{2} \times 4$	A	Sun	Green, red	Spring	G.C
armenum	,,	,,	2×8	,,	,,	Green, purple	,,	,,
ballsii	,,	,,	2×6	,,	,,	Bronze	,,	,,
borissovae	,,	,,	2×8	,,	,,	Deep green, brown	,,	,,
calcaratum	,,	,,	3×8	,,	,,	Deep brown, red	,,	,,
cantabricum	,,	,,	2×6	,,	,,	Deep green, brown	,,	,,
caucasicum	,,	,,	2×6	,,	,,	Green, brown	,,	,,
ciliosum	,,	,,	1×6	,,	,,	Grey-green	,,	,,
borisii	,,	,,	1×6	,,	,,	Grey-green, white	,,	,,
Ali Botusch form	,,	,,	1×6	,,	,,	Green, red	,,	,,
Mali Hat form	,,	,,	1×6	,,	,,	Plum, red	,,	,,
dolomiticum	,,	,,	1×6	,,	,,	Light green, red	,,	,,
erythraeum	,,	,,	1×6	,,	,,	Green, red	,,	,,
Pirin form	,,	,,	1×6	,,	,,	Green	,,	,,
giuseppii	,,	,,	2×8	,,	,,	Light green, red	,,	,,
globiferum	,,	,,	2×8	,,	,,	Yellow green	,,	,,
grandiflorum	,,	,,	2×8	,,	,,	Green, brown	,,	,,
heuffelii	,,	,,	2×8	,,	,,	Green, red	,,	,,
hirtum	,,	,,	1×8	,,	,,	Yellowish-green, red	,,	,,
ingwersenii	,,	,,	2×8	,,	,,	Green, brown	,,	,,
kindingeri	,,	,,	2×8	,,	,,	Light green, red	,,	,,

Name of Plant	Suitability	Type	Height and spread in inches	Soil	Position and Protection	Colour and Season		Propagation
SEMPERVIVUM (*cont.*)								
kosaninii	B	H.E	2×8	A	Sun	Deep green, brown	Spring	G.C
Koprivnik	,,	,,	2×6	,,	,,	Light green, brown	,,	,,
leucanthum	,,	,,	2×8	,,	,,	Pale green, brown	,,	,,
macedonicum	,,	,,	2×8	,,	,,	Green	,,	,,
marmoreum	,,	,,	2×8	,,	,,	Green, brown	,,	,,
brunneifolium	,,	,,	2×8	,,	,,	Brown	,,	,,
rubrifolium	,,	,,	2×8	,,	,,	Red, green	,,	,,
ornatum (syn. S. ornatum)	,,	,,	2×8	,,	,,	Rich red, green	,,	,,
minus	,,	,,	1×6	,,	,,	Olive, brown	,,	,,
glabrum	,,	,,	1×6	,,	,,	Green, bronze	,,	,,
montanum	,,	,,	1×6	,,	,,	Dull green	,,	,,
burnatii	,,	,,	2×6	,,	,,	Light green	,,	,,
nevadense	,,	,,	2×6	,,	,,	Red	,,	,,
octopodes	,,	,,	1×6	,,	,,	Green, brown	,,	,,
ossetiense	,,	,,	2×6	,,	,,	Green, brown	,,	,,
pittonii	,,	,,	1×6	,,	,,	Dull green, purple	,,	,,
pumilum	,,	,,	1×6	,,	,,	Light green	,,	,,
Elbruz form	,,	,,	1×6	,,	,,	Light green, red	,,	,,
reginae-amaliae	,,	,,	2×6	,,	,,	Dull green, purple	,,	,,
soboliferum	,,	,,	1×6	,,	,,	Green, red	,,	,,

Name of Plant	Suita-bility	Type	Height and spread in inches	Soil	Position and Protection	Colour and Season		Propa-gation
tectorum	B	H.E	2×8	A	Sun	Green, purple	Spring	G.C
alpinum	,,	,,	1×6	,,	,,	Green, purple	,,	,,
calcareum	,,	,,	2×8	,,	,,	Green, brown	,,	,,
Dr Giuseppi	,,	,,	2×8	,,	,,	Green, red	,,	,,
thompsonianum	,,	,,	1×6	,,	,,	Yellow, green, red	,,	,,
×*versicolor*	,,	,,	2×8	,,	,,	Green, purple	,,	,,
wulfenii	,,	,,	2×8	,,	,,	Green	,,	,,
zelebori	,,	,,	2×8	,,	,,	Green, brown	,,	,,

A last word on Sempervivums: buy only from a reputable source for the hybrids and seedlings are innumerable and their ease of propagation has assisted in spreading many worthless forms under names of true species.

Name of Plant	Suita-bility	Type	Height and spread in inches	Soil	Position and Protection	Colour and Season		Propa-gation
HORTIA								
galacifolia	C	S.S.E	6×6	C.N	S	White	April	D
uniflora	,,	,,	4×6	,,	,,	Pink	,,	,,
grandiflora	,,	,,	4×6	,,	,,	,,	,,	,,
rosea	,,	,,	4×6	,,	,,	Deep rose	,,	,,
ILENE								
acaulis	B	H.E	2×6	A	Sun	Rose-pink	May	D.S
alba	,,	,,	2×6	,,	,,	White	,,	,,
elongata	,,	,,	2×6	,,	,,	Bright pink	,,	,,
alpestris	A	,,	4×6	,,	H.S	White	,,	S
flore pleno	,,	,,	4×6	,,	,,	,,	,,	D
keiskei	B	H.P	3×4	,,	Sun	Rose-pink	June	S
pusilla	,,	H.E	2×4	,,	,,	White	May	,,
schafta	,,	,,	4×6	,,	,,	Rose	Aug.	,,
SOLDANELLA								
alpina	,,	,,	3×6	B	,,	Lavender-blue	Mar.	D.S
minima	,,	,,	2×4	,,	,,	Lilac	,,	,,
montana	,,	,,	4×6	,,	,,	Lavender	,,	,,

Name of Plant	Suita-bility	Type	Height and spread in inches	Soil	Position and Protection	Colour and Season		Propa-gation
SOLDANELLA (*cont.*)								
pindicola	B	H.E	6×6	B	Sun	Lilac	April	D.S
pusilla	,,	,,	3×4	,,	,,	Pale pink	Mar.	,,
SPIRAEA								
caespitosa	See *Petrophytum caespitosum*							
hendersonii	See *Petrophytum hendersonii*							
STATICE								
gougetiana	See *Limonium gougetianum*							
STERNBERGIA								
fischeriana	A	B	5×4	B	Sun	Yellow	Feb.	D
lutea	,,	,,	5×4	,,	,,	,,	Sept.	,,
SYNTHYRIS								
rotundifolia sweetzeri	,,	H.E	4×6	,,	,,	Deep violet	Feb.	,,
stellata	,,	,,	4×6	,,	,,	Pale violet	Mar.	,,
TALINUM								
okanoganense	B	H.P	1×3	A	,,	White	May	S
TANAKAEA								
radicans	C	H.E	4×6	B	S	,,	,,	D
TEUCRIUM								
marum	A	S.E	6×8	A	Sun	Red	July	G.C
polium	,,	,,	4×6	,,	,,	Golden	,,	,,
pyrenaicum	,,	,,	2×6	,,	,,	Cream and lilac	,,	,,
roseum	,,	,,	2×6	,,	,,	Cream and purple	,,	,,
subspinosum	,,	,,	8×5	,,	,,	Lilac	,,	,,
THALICTRUM								
alpinum	,,	H.P	6×6	,,	,,	Yellow	June	D
kiusianum	,,	,,	4×6	,,	H.S	Mauve	,,	,,
THLASPI								
rotundifolium	B	H.E	2×6	D	Sun	Lilac	May	G.C
stylosum	,,	,,	2×6	A	,,	Rose-lilac	Mar.	S

Name of Plant	Suita-bility	Type	Height and spread in inches	Soil	Position and Protection	Colour and Season		Propa-gation
THYMUS								
caespititius	B	S.E	2×12	A	Sun	Lilac-blue	July	G.C
carnosus	,,	,,	6×6	,,	,,	Pink	June	,,
doerfleri	,,	,,	6×12	,,	,,	Deep pink	,,	,,
herba-barona	,,	,,	3×6	,,	,,	,,	,,	,,
integer	,,	,,	1×6	,,	Sun P	Lilac-pink	May	,,
longiflorus	,,	,,	6×6	,,	,,	Lilac-purple	June	,,
membranaceus	,,	,,	4×8	,,	Sun	White	,,	,,
nitidus	,,	,,	6×8	,,	,,	Lilac-pink	,,	,,
villosus	,,	,,	2×6	,,	,,	Rosy-purple	,,	D
TOWNSENDIA								
grandiflora	,,	H.E	6×6	,,	H.S	Violet	May	S
wilcoxiana	,,	,,	2×4	,,	,,	Lavender-blue	,,	,,
TRACHELIUM								
asperuloides (syn. *Diosphaera asperuloides*)	,,	H.P	1×6	D	Sun	Slate blue	June	G.C
TRADESCANTIA								
rosea graminea	A	,,	3×3	A	H.S	Rose-pink	,,	D
TRIFOLIUM								
alpinum	,,	,,	3×6	,,	Sun	Lilac-pink	May	S
uniflorum	,,	H.E	2×8	,,	,,	Red and cream	June	,,
TRILLIUM								
undulatum	,,	H.P	6×6	,,	S	White and purple	May	D
TULIPA								
australis	B	B	6×3	B	Sun	Yellow and red	April	D.S
biflora	,,	,,	6×3	,,	,,	Cream	,,	,,
hageri	,,	,,	6×3	,,	,,	Copper red	,,	,,
humilis	,,	,,	5×3	,,	,,	Pale purple	,,	,,

Name of Plant	Suita-bility	Type	Height and spread in inches	Soil	Position and Protection	Colour and Season		Propa-gation
TULIPA (*cont.*)								
linifolia	B	B	6×3	B	Sun	Crimson	May	D.S
persica	,,	,,	6×4	,,	Sun	Yellow	May	S
tarda	,,	,,	4×6	,,	,,	,,	April	D
turkestanica	,,	,,	6×6	,,	,,	,,	,,	,,
wilsoniana	,,	,,	6×4	,,	,,	Crimson	May	S
VACCINIUM								
caespitosum	C	S.D	6×8	C.N	S	Rose-pink	May	S.C
						Black	Sept.	
delavayi	,,	S.E	6×8	,,	,,	Pale pink	May	,,
						Black	Sept.	
deliciosum	,,	S.D	9×9	,,	,,	Pink	May	,,
						Black	Sept.	
macrocarpum	,,	S.E	4×9	,,	,,	Pink	May	,,
						Red	Sept.	
myrtilloides	,,	S.D	6×9	,,	,,	White	May	,,
						Black	Sept.	
praestans	,,	,,	4×9	,,	,,	White	June	,,
						Red	Sept.	,,

VERONICA

Numerous species formerly known as veronicas are now referred to as hebe and are described under the genus *Hebe*.

armena	A	S.S.E	2×9	A	Sun	Blue	June	C
bombycina	,,	H.E	3×6	,,	Sun P	China blue	May	G.C
canescens	,,	,,	1×9	,,	Sun	Pale blue	June	D
cinerea	,,	,,	6×8	,,	,,	,,	,,	,,
filifolia	,,	H.P	4×6	,,	,,	China blue	,,	D
telephilifolia	,,	,,	1×6	,,	,,	China blue	July	,,

VIOLA

aetolica	,,	H.E	2×4	,,	,,	Yellow	May	S
biflora	,,	H.P	3×6	,,	,,	Golden	April	,,
blanda	,,	,,	2×6	,,	,,	White	,,	,,
delphinantha	,,	S.S.D	3×3	,,	,,	Rose-lilac	May	G.C
pedata	,,	H.P	4×6	,,	,,	Pale lilac	,,	D
yakusimana	,,	,,	½×3	,,	,,	White and lavender	,,	S

Name of Plant	Suita-bility	Type	Height and spread in inches	Soil	Position and Protection	Colour and Season		Propa-gation
ISCARIA (syn. LYCHNIS)								
alpina	B	H.E	4×4	A.N	Sun	Bright rose	May	S
lagascae	A	,,	6×4	,,	,,	Rose-pink	June	,,
AHLENBERGIA								
matthewsii	B	,,	6×8	,,	,,	Lilac	July	,,
saxicola	,,	H.E	3×6	,,	,,	White	May	,,

Name of plant	Suita-bility	Type	Height and spread in inches	Soil	Position and Protection	Colour and Season		Propa-gation
ANEMONE								
magellanica	B	H.P	6 × 6	B.N	Sun	Cream	May	S
,, *lesseri*	,,	,,	6 × 6	,,	,,	Red	April	,,
obtusiloba	C	,,	3 × 9	C	H.S	Blue	June	,,
AQUILEGIA								
akitensis	A	,,	6 × 5	B	A	Deep blue	May	,,
ARTEMISIA								
schmidtiana nana	,,	E	3 × 9	A	Sun	Silver foliage	May	G.C
ASPERULA								
nitida puberula	B	,,	1 × 6	,,	,,	Light pink	May	,,
CALCEOLARIA								
Walter Shrimpton	,,	,,	3 × 9	B	,,	Gold and maroon	June	,,
CAMPANULA								
carpatha	A	,,	3 × 9	A	,,	Pale violet-blue	June	S
formanekiana	,,	,,	12 × 12	A.N	,,	White	June	,,
isophylla	,,	,,	6 × 12	,,	,,	Blue	July	G.C
,, *alba*	,,	,,	6 × 12	,,	,,	White	,,	,,
pilosa alba	,,	H.E	4 × 6	,,	Sun C	,,	June	S
planiflora	,,	E	6 × 8	B	Sun	Light blue	June	G.C. S
,, *alba*	,,	,,	6 × 8	,,	,,	White	June	C.G
CASSIOPE								
Badenoch	C	S.E	7 × 8	C.N	S	White	May	,,
Bearsden	,,	,,	6 × 8	,,	,,	,,	,,	,,
Edinburgh	,,	,,	8 × 10	,,	,,	,,	,,	,,
Muirhead	,,	,,	8 × 12	,,	,,	,,	,,	,,
Randle Cooke	,,	,,	8 × 10	,,	,,	,,	,,	,,
CELMISIA								
du-rietzii	A	H.E	6 × 10	A	Sun	,,	June	S
gracilenta	,,	,,	6 × 10	,,	,,	,,	,,	,,
incana	,,	,,	5 × 10	,,	,,	,,	,,	,,
CERASTIUM								
alpinum lanatum	A	E	3 × 10	A.C	Sun	White	May	S

Name of plant	Suita-bility	Type	Height and spread in inches	Soil	Position and Protection	Colour and Season		Propa-gation
CONANDRON								
ramondioides	C	H.P	3 × 8	C.N	S	Violet	June	,,
CONVOLVULUS								
incanus	A	E	3 × 12	A.N	Sun	Pink	,,	D
mauritanicus	,,	H.P	6 × 15	,,	,,	Lilac-blue	,,	S
CROCUS								
flavus	,,	B	3 × 3	A	,,	Orange	March	S.D
vernus	,,	,,	3 × 3	,,	,,	Orange-yellow	March	,,
CYATHODES								
colensoi	C	S.E	12 × 12	C	,,	Cream	April	R.C
CYTISUS								
procumbens	A	S.D	6 × 18	A	,,	Deep yellow	May	C
DIANTHUS								
alpinus	A	H.E	2 × 4	A.C	Sun	Deep rose-pink	June	S. G.C
alpinus albus	,,	,,	2 × 4	,,	,,	White	,,	,,
arvernensis	,,	,,	2 × 6	A.N	,,	Deep pink	July	S
brachyanthus var. *viscidus*	,,	,,	2 × 8	A.N	,,	Pink	June	,,
Elizabeth	,,	,,	3 × 9	A.C	,,	Deep pink	July	C
strictus	,,	,,	6 × 10	A.C	,,	,,	May	S
DICENTRA								
cucullaria	B	H.P	3 × 5	B.N	H.S	Pale pink	May	D
oregana	,,	,,	6 × 6	,,	,,	Rose	April	,,
DIONYSIA								
aretioides	,,	H.E	2 × 6	D	,,	Yellow	,,	S. G.C
DISPORUM								
smithii	C	H.P	6 × 9	C	,,	Greeny-white	May	
						Orange	Sept.	S
DODECATHEON								
pauciflorum	A	,,	9 × 6	B.N	,,	Lilac	May	S.D
ERIGERON								
simplex	,,	E	3 × 8	A	Sun	Violet-blue	,,	S

Name of plant	Suita-bility	Type	Height and spread in inches	Soil	Position and Protection	Colour and Season		Propa-gation
ΛANKENIA								
aevis	,,	E	1 × 10	A.N	Sun	Pink	July	G.C
ITILLARIA								
yrenaica	B	B	12 × 3	A.N	,,	Mottled brownish-green	May	D
EBE								
Carl Teschner	A	SE	6 × 9	A	,,	Violet-blue	June	G.C
Cranleighensis	,,	,,	12 × 12	,,	,,	Pink	,,	,,
Cranleigh Gem	,,	,,	9 × 9	,,	,,	White	,,	,,
ELICHRYSUM								
ibthorpii	,,	,,	9 × 9	,,	,,	,,	,,	C
ELONIOPSIS								
rientalis *ar. yakusimensis*	C	E	3 × 6	C	H.S	White to violet	April	D
UCOJUM								
estivum	,,	B	9 × 2	,,	,,	White	,,	D.S
OMOCHARIS								
airei	,,	,,	9 × 4	,,	,,	Light pink, spotted purple	May	S.D
KALIS								
nneaphylla minuta	B	,,	1 × 8	B	Sun	Pink	,,	D
aciniata	B	,,	1 × 6	,,	,,	Lavender-blue, veined purple	June	,,
NSTEMON								
ampanulatus pulchellus	A	S.E	1 × 8	A	,,	Purple, violet, blue	June	G.C
couleri	,,	,,	3 × 9	,,	,,	Lilac	,,	,,
,, albus	,,	,,	3 × 9	,,	,,	White	,,	,,
ERIS								
aponica *Variegata*	C	S.E	18 × 12	C	H.S	White	April	R.C

Name of plant	Suita-bility	Type	Height and spread in inches	Soil	Position and Protection	Colour and Season		Propagation
PLATYCODON								
grandiflorum Apoyana	A	H.P	9×6	B	Sun	Blue	August	S
POTENTILLA								
eriocarpa	,,	E	1×8	A	,,	Yellow	,,	C.S
fruticosa var. *mandschurica*	,,	S.D	6×9	N.A	,,	White	June	C
PRIMULA (European)								
marginata Caerulea	B	H.E	4×6	A.L	Sun	Deep lavender-blue	May	C
PRIMULA (Asiatic)								
modesta	A	H.P	3×6	C	S.P	Rose	April	S
petiolaris	,,	,,	3×6	,,	,,	Rich pink	,,	S.D
rosea	B	,,	6×8	,,	,,	Rose-pink	May	S
PULSATILLA								
halleri slavica	A	,,	6×8	A.L	Sun	Purple-rose	April	,,
RANUNCULUS								
insignis	,,	H	4×6	A.N	,,	Yellow	May	,,
SAXIFRAGA								
Southside Seedling	,,	E	3×9	A	,,	White, red centre	,,	C
SPIRAEA								
bullata Nana	,,	S.E	4×10	,,	,,	Deep rose	June	R.C
TROLLIUS								
pumilus	B	H.P	6×8	B	,,	Deep yellow	,,	S
TULIPA								
aucheriana	A	B	3×3	A	,,	Pink, striped yellow	April	D.S
VIOLA								
cornata alba	,,	B	2×6	,,	,,	White	May	S

NOMENCLATURE CHANGES

Since the second edition of this book was published in 1969 numerous botanical name changes have been made. Those on the left are the names given in the body of the text; those on the right are the currently valid names:

Juniperus commumis Echiniformis = *Juniperus chinensis* Echiniformis.

Aethionema creticum = *Aethionema saxatile*.

Alyssum spinosum = *Ptilotrichum spinosum*.

Alyssum spinosum Roseum = *Ptilotrichum spinosum* Roseum.

Androsace charpentieri = *Androsace brevis*.

Androsace imbricata = *Androsace vandellii*.

Armeria caespitosa = *Armeria juniperifolia*.

Artemisia mutellina = *Artemisia umbelliformis*.

Boykinia jamesii = *Telesonix jamesii*.

Campanula abietina = *Campanula patula abietina*.

Campanula caespitosa = *Campanula cespitosa*.

Celsia acaulis = *Verbascum acaulis*.

Crocus salzmannii = *Crocus serotinus* subsp. *salzmannii*

Crocus susianus = *Crocus augustifolius*.

Cyclamen europaeum = *Cyclamen purpurascens*.

Cyclamen hiemale = *Cyclamen coum*.

Cyclamen ibericum = *Cyclamen coum*.

Cytisus demissus = *Chamaecytisus hirsutus*.

Dianthus neglectus = *Dianthus pavonius*.

Dianthus noeanus = *Dianthus petraeus noeanus*.

Dianthus pindicola = *Dianthus haematocalyx pindicola*.

Erodium chamaedryoides = *Erodium reichardii*.

Genista dalmatica = *Genista sylvestris* (local form).

Genista delphinensis = *Chamaespartium delphinensis*.

Genista patula = *Genista tinctoria* (local form).

Genista villarsii = *Genista pulchella*.

Geranium subcaulescens = *Geranium cinereum subcaulescens*.

Globularia nana = *Globularia repens*.

Hypericum repens = *Hypericum linarioides*.

Hypericum rhodopeum = *Hypericum cerastoides*.

Iberis jordanii = *Iberis pruitii*.

Iberis taurica = *Iberis simplex*.

Iberis tenoreana = *Iberis pruitii*.

Iris mellita = *Iris suaveolens*.

Iris pumila cretica = *Iris cretensis*.

Leucojum hiemale = *Leucojum nicacense*.

Linaria aequitriloba = *Cymbalaria aequitriloba*.

Lithospermum oleifelium = *Lithodora oleifolia*.

Micromeria piperella = *Micromeria marginata*.

Minuartia aretioides = *Minuartia cherlerioides*.

Myosotis rupicola = *Myosotis alpestris* (dwarf form).

Narcissus bulbocodium tenuifolius = *Narcissus bulbocodium* subsp. *bulbocodium*

Narcissus cernuus = *Narcissus triandrus* subsp. *triandrus*

Narcissus juncifolius = *Narcissus requienii*.

Narcissus juncifolius rupicola = *Narcissus rupicola*.

Narcissus pallidus praecox = *Narcissus triandrus* subsp. *pallidulus.*

Narcissus triandrus calathinus = *Narcissus requienii.*

Narcissus triandrus concolor = *Narcissus triandrus* subsp. *pallidulus.*

Narcissus triandrus pulchellus = *Narcissus triandrus* subsp. *triandrus.*

Passerina nivalis = *Thymelaea nivalis.*

Phlox nana var. *ensifolia* = *Phlox triovulata.*

Phyteuma comosum = *Physoplexis comosa.*

Phyteuma halleri = *Phyteuma ovatum.*

Phyteuma pauciflorum = *Phyteuma globulariifolium.*

Potentilla verna = *Potentilla taberaemontani.*

Primula auricula ciliata = *Primula ciliata.*

Primula longifolia = *Primula halleri.*

Primula rubra = *Primula viscosa.*

Raoulia australis = *Raoulia hookeri.*

Raoulia lutescens = *Raoulia australis.*

Rhododendron myrtilloides = *Rhododendron campylogynum myrtilloides.*

Rhodohypoxis baurii = *Rhodohypoxis baurei.*

Saxifraga boryi = *Saxifraga marginata.*

Saxifraga burseriana = *Saxifraga burserana.*

Saxifraga lingulata = *Saxifraga callosa lingulata.*

Saxifraga sancta = *Saxifraga juniperifolia sancta.*

Schizocodon soldanelloides = *Shortia soldanelloides.*

Schizocodon magnus = *Shortia soldanelloides magnus.*

Sempervivum allionii = *Jovibarba allionii.*

Sempervivum arenarium = *Sempervivum arenaria.*

Sempervivum heuffelii = *Jovibarba heuffelii.*

Sempervivum hirtum = *Sempervivum hirta.*

Sempervivum soboliferum = *Jovibarba sobolifera.*

Sempervivum zelebori = *Sempervivum zeleborii.*

Thymus nitidus = *Thymus richardii nitidus.*

Tulipa australis = *Tulipa sylvestris* subsp. *australis*

Tulipa hageri = *Tulipa orphanidea.*

Viscaria alpina = *Lychnis alpina.*

Viscaria lagascae = *Lychnis lagascae.*

METRIC/IMPERIAL CONVERSION SCALE

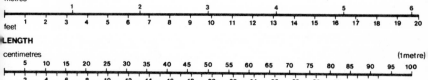

metres

| 1 | 2 | 3 | 4 | 5 | 6 |

feet 1 2 3 4 5 6 7 8 9 10 11 12 13 14 15 16 17 18 19 20

LENGTH

centimetres (1 metre)

5 10 15 20 25 30 35 40 45 50 55 60 65 70 75 80 85 90 95 100

inches 2 4 6 8 10 12 (1ft) 14 16 18 20 22 24 (2ft) 26 28 30 32 34 36 (l yd)

INDEX

ADDITIONS TO LIST OF PLANTS

Name of plant	Suita-bility	Type	Height and spread in inches	Soil	Position and Protection	Colour and Season		Propa-gation
ACHILLEA								
ageratifolia	A	E	4×6	A	Sun	White	June	C
clavenae	,,	E	6×6	,,	,,	,,	July	RC
umbellata	,,	E	4×6	,,	,,	,,	,,	,,
ADONIS								
amurensis	,,	H.P.	9×9	A.L	,,	Golden	March	S
vernalis	,,	,,	9×9	,,	,,	Golden-yellow	April	,,
AETHIONEMA								
coridifolium	,,	E	6×8	,,	,,	Bright pink	May	G.C.
grandiflorum	,,	,,	10×12	,,	,,	Deep pink	June	,,
iberideum	,,	,,	6×12	,,	,,	White	March	,,
pulchellum	,,	,,	8×9	,,	,,	Pink	May	,,
ALLIUM								
anceps	,,	B	5×4	A	,,	Pale pink	August	S
ALYSSUM								
serpyllifolium	,,	S.E	2×9	,,	,,	Golden-yellow	June	C
ANACYCLUS								
depressus	,,	E	3×9	,,	,,	White, red reverse	May	S
ANAGALLIS								
collina	,,	E	3×9	A.N	,,	Orange-scarlet	May	G.C
tenella	,,	H.P	1×10	B.N	,,	Pale pink	June	D
ANDROSACE								
alpina	B	E	1×4	D	H.S	Pink	April	S
lanuginosa	A	,,	3×9	A.N	Sun	Lilac	June	G.C
sarmentosa	,,	,,	3×9	,,	,,	Bright pink	July	,,
villosa taurica	B	,,	1×6	D	,,	White	April	S